SCOTTISH HIGHER HIS

APPEASEMENT
and the
ROAD to WAR

David Armstrong
Elizabeth Trueland

HODDER
GIBSON
AN HACHETTE UK COMPANY

The Publishers would like to thank the following for permission to reproduce copyright material:

Photo credits

Deutsches Historisches Museum (page 2); Will Dyson, Daily Herald, 13th May 1919 / Centre for the Study of Cartoons and Caricature, University of Kent, Canterbury (page 6); David Low, The Star, 19 Aug 1924 / Solo Syndication / Centre for the Study of Cartoons and Caricature, University of Kent, Canterbury (page 11); Deutsches Historisches Museum (page 12 both); Akg-images (page 16); Landesbildstelle, Berlin (page 21); David Low, Evening Standard, 2nd October 1933 / Solo Syndication / Centre for the Study of Cartoons and Caricature, University of Kent, Canterbury (page 23); MARY EVANS/WEIMAR ARCHIVE (page 25); Deutsches Historisches Museum (page 31); Peace Pledge Union (page 33); © Bettmann/CORBIS (page 34); Reproduced with Permission of Punch Ltd., www.punch.co.uk (page 44); David Low, Evening Standard, 07 Mar 1938 / Solo Syndication / Centre for the Study of Cartoons and Caricature, University of Kent, Canterbury (page 45); Fox Photos / Hulton Archive /Getty Images (page 51); David Low, Evening Standard, 08 Jul 1936/ Solo Syndication / Centre for the Study of Cartoons and Caricature, University of Kent, Canterbury (page 55); Akg-images (page 62); Akg-images (page 64); Akg-images (page 69); © Hulton-Deutsch Collection/CORBIS (page 75); David Low, Evening Standard, 18th February 1938 / Solo Syndication / Centre for the Study of Cartoons and Caricature, University of Kent, Canterbury (page 79); © Hulton-Deutsch Collection/CORBIS (page 81); © Hulton-Deutsch Collection/CORBIS (page 82); David Low, Evening Standard, 12th April 1938 / Solo Syndication / Centre for the Study of Cartoons and Caricature, University of Kent, Canterbury (page 86); Mary Evans Picture Library (page 91); © Hulton-Deutsch Collection/CORBIS (page 92); © Bettmann/CORBIS (page 94); © Bettmann/CORBIS (page 102); © CORBIS (page 106); Mary Evans Picture Library (page 107); akg-images / IMS (page 118); © Bettmann/CORBIS (page 125).

Index supplied by Indexing Specialists (UK) Ltd.

Every effort has been made to trace all copyright holders, but if any have been inadvertently overlooked the Publishers will be pleased to make the necessary arrangements at the first opportunity.

Although every effort has been made to ensure that website addresses are correct at time of going to press, Hodder Gibson cannot be held responsible for the content of any website mentioned in this book. It is sometimes possible to find a relocated web page by typing in the address of the home page for a website in the URL window of your browser.

Orders: please contact Bookpoint Ltd, 130 Milton Park, Abingdon, Oxon OX14 4SB. Telephone: (44) 01235 827720. Fax: (44) 01235 400454. Lines are open from 9.00–5.00, Monday to Saturday, with a 24-hour message answering service. Visit our website at www.hoddereducation.co.uk. Hodder Gibson can be contacted direct on: Tel: 0141 848 1609; Fax: 0141 889 6315; email: hoddergibson@hodder.co.uk

Contents

Contents

Introduction

Who this book is for

It is for anyone taking Higher History and in particular the Later Modern period, which is the option studied by the vast majority of students.

Why was this book written?

It was written to provide an easy-to-read textbook for students who are aiming not just to pass their exam but to pass well. Other books are either difficult to read and contain far too much content, only provide basic information in pass notes style or are not written specifically for the Scottish Higher History course. This is the first full and accessible textbook series for this part of the Higher History course.

What is in this book?

It covers all you need to know about the section on Appeasement and the Road to War in the Later Modern option of your Higher History course. All of the syllabus is covered so you can be sure all your needs will be met. Read on to find out the content covered.

Why are there various activities at the end of each chapter?

Research in learning proves that if you just read as a means of learning, after 24 hours you will only have retained about 10 per cent of the new information. Unless learning is reinforced it does not become anchored in either your short-term or long-term memory.

If, after reading, you attempt an activity which requires you to use the information you have read and process it in a different way than it was presented in this book then your memory will retain over 60 per cent of your reading. That is why each chapter has an activity, the intention of which is to provide effective learning techniques to help acquire and reinforce knowledge. These activities can be applied to any topic with some slight adjustments.

Appeasement

On September 1st 1939, the armies of Nazi Germany invaded Poland. Two days later, Britain and France declared war on Hitler's Germany. The Second World War had begun. Almost exactly twenty years earlier, the 'Great War for Civilisation' had ended at the Paris Peace Conferences. To most Europeans, the thought of another conflict was unbelievable. How

had this happened? Why did the leaders and populations of Europe find themselves at war again?

It is the purpose of this book to try to answer these questions. The authors will trace the beginnings of the trouble by looking at how and why the British government followed a policy of appeasement. This word is defined in Chambers Dictionary as:

> *to pacify; to placate by making or effecting concessions; to satisfy; to quiet; to allay; appeasement – the action of appeasing*

Appeasement could be said to have begun almost from the moment that the Treaty of Versailles was signed. Certainly, the roots of the policy pursued by the British government towards Hitler's Germany in the 1930s, can be traced to this.

An understanding of the ideas of fascism is also important, especially how they affected the foreign policies of Italy under Mussolini and Nazi Germany led by Adolf Hitler. The failure of the policy of collective security through the League of Nations will also be considered.

The core of this book covers what you must know to be successful in this course:

- Hitler's reoccupation of the Rhineland in March 1936.
- Foreign intervention in the Spanish Civil War.
- The German invasion of Austria (*Anschluss*).
- The crisis over Czechoslovakia, leading to the Munich agreement in Autumn 1938.

All the sources and questions in Paper II of the Higher examination concentrate on these core topics. However, to complete the story of appeasement and to fully understand the historical debates surrounding it, we also need to examine what happened after Munich and relate this to the outbreak of war in September 1939. At the end of each chapter, there are a number of tasks. At least two of them will be very similar to those found in the final examination in dealing with questions regarding sources. The authors hope that the text and the tasks following will prepare you thoroughly for this. To help you through these, a model answer/worked example of each of the five different types of questions found in the exam has been provided for you. Other tasks should enhance your knowledge and understanding of this hugely important topic.

1 The legacy of World War One

Introduction

On 11 November 1918, the bloodbath that was World War One finally ended. Countless millions hoped that this had indeed been 'the war to end all wars'. When the peacemakers gathered in Paris in January 1919 they aimed to draw up a peace settlement which would ensure that there would never be another war on the scale of the one that had just ended.

At the same time, they had to deal with the break-up of three great empires: the Austro–Hungarian Empire, the Turkish Empire and the Russian Empire. Additionally, the Bolshevik take-over in Russia in November 1917 had alarmed the ruling classes across Europe and the peacemakers were determined to halt the spread of communism.

It soon became clear that there was no simple solution to the problem of ensuring future peace and, despite the efforts of the peacemakers, the various treaties signed in June 1919 created as many problems as they solved. Historians may no longer blame the peacemakers of 1919 for everything that went wrong in the 1920s and 1930s, but nevertheless Hitler's popularity was founded at least in part on his determination to overthrow the most famous of the treaties, the Treaty of Versailles.

The determination to guarantee a peaceful future also led to the creation of the League of Nations. But despite the optimism that surrounded its creation, by the early 1930s it was clear that the League could not guarantee security in the face of outright aggression.

Resentment among the defeated powers

The defeated powers, and particularly Germany, felt aggrieved by the way in which they were treated at the Paris Peace Conference. Germany was not allowed to take part in the discussions, and the terms of the peace were largely dictated by the 'Big Three' victorious powers – Britain, France and the USA.

Source 1.1

Post-war Europe, 1919

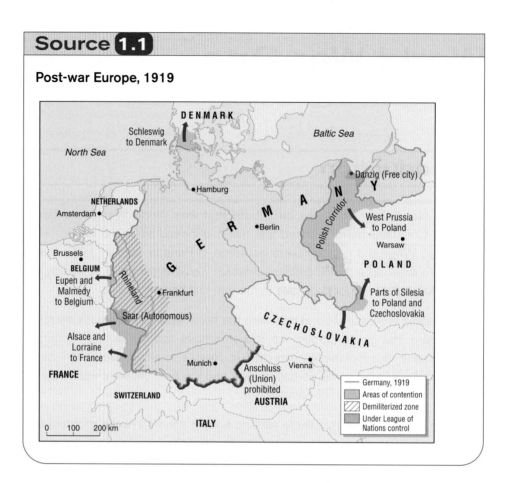

By the terms of the Treaty of Versailles, Germany lost land, resources and population; and all of its overseas colonies were put under League of Nations control. In addition, Germany was forced to disarm: the German army was reduced to 100,000 men, the German navy was reduced, submarines were banned and Germany was not allowed to have an air force.

Germany was also forced to accept Article 231, the War Guilt Clause, which stated that Germany, with its ally, Austria–Hungary, was responsible for starting the war. Since Germany was held responsible for the outbreak of war, it was also held responsible for the damage caused by the fighting, and would be forced to pay reparations.

The Treaty of Versailles had enormous economic repercussions

Source 1.2

German poster showing the impact of the Versailles Treaty

for Germany. The final bill for reparations (compensation to be paid to the victorious allies) amounted to £6.6bn. The treaty also forbade union with Austria, so that there was no possibility of creating a new German super-state.

In September 1919, Austria signed a separate treaty with the Allies, the Treaty of Saint-Germain. The new republic of Austria was now completely independent from the other parts of the old Habsburg Empire, and the South Tyrol, a German-speaking area, was transferred to Italy. From the start, the new Austria suffered major economic problems and was politically divided, with right-wing parties still looking to closer ties with Germany.

The new states of central and eastern Europe

One of the major problems the peacemakers of 1919 faced was that the map of Europe had in effect already been redrawn as new states declared their independence in the final months of the war. But defining the frontiers of these new states did not prove easy because of the widespread ethnic mix across the whole region. After 1919, there were large numbers of ethnic Germans living in Poland, Czechoslovakia and Hungary, as well as other German-speaking communities in Romania, Yugoslavia and western Russia.

The Germans were not unique. There were other ethnic minorities scattered through eastern Europe including Poles, Slovaks, Jews, Serbs and Croats, as well as the Roma, or gypsies. The existence of so many different ethnic minorities across Europe provided a focal point for extremists throughout the interwar period. At the same time, many western European political leaders acknowledged that some of these ethnic grievances were justified and looked for ways to remedy the most obvious of them.

The League of Nations and collective security

The League of Nations was established in 1920 as part of the peacemaking process. Its aim was 'to promote international co-operation and to achieve international peace and security' by committing member states to work together to maintain the peace. League members also agreed to disarm 'to the lowest point consistent with national safety', although the lowest point consistent with national safety was never satisfactorily defined. At the heart of the League was the commitment to collective security. If one member was attacked, then all other members would act together to come to the aid of the member under attack.

Source 1.3

German-speaking peoples 1919–39

In a crisis the League could react in a number of ways. Most of these aimed to resolve disputes without using force. However, if one member state attacked another, the League would impose a range of diplomatic and economic sanctions on the aggressor. If these sanctions failed, the League could recommend military sanctions.

In total, more than sixty countries were at one time League members, but the League was undermined because it never represented all of the world's major powers. Germany was only admitted to the League in 1926 and withdrew in 1933, while the USSR did not become a member until 1934. The USA never joined.

Britain, France and collective security

In the early 1920s Britain and France differed in their attitudes towards both the Treaty of Versailles and the League of Nations. As a result, relations between the two countries were not particularly good.

France remained deeply suspicious of Germany. France was not prepared to discuss disarmament and continued to maintain a large army as well as the largest air force in the world at the time. In addition, France aimed, as far as possible, to 'encircle' Germany with allies, and consequently the French entered into a series of defensive alliances with Poland (1921), Czechoslovakia (1924), Romania (1926) and Yugoslavia (1927). The existence of these treaties undermined the concept of collective security because it was clear that the French did not feel that it could rely solely on the League of Nations.

Britain's attitude did little to reassure the French. In the early 1920s, the two powers differed over the enforcement of the Treaty of Versailles, particularly when the French occupied the Ruhr, in response to Germany's failure to make reparation payments. Unlike France, Britain hoped that the League would provide a way of resolving international disputes arising out of the Peace Treaties, through negotiation and boundary adjustments if necessary. Britain was also suspicious of French efforts to strengthen collective security, fearing that it might lead to British involvement in European disputes, which the government believed the country could not afford.

By the mid 1920s, however, the two main League powers were working together better and for a few years there was genuine optimism that the League, now with Germany on board, would prove a valuable means of keeping the peace.

League failure in Manchuria

In September 1931 the League of Nations faced a major crisis when the Japanese Army occupied large areas of Manchuria, which was part of China. Both China and Japan were League members and the Chinese government quickly appealed to the League. It was agreed that the League of Nations would set up a commission of inquiry, but six months elapsed before the Commission set off for Manchuria. While the League delayed, the Japanese established a new puppet state in Manchuria, which was renamed Manchukuo. When the League eventually condemned the invasion of Manchuria, Japan announced its withdrawal from the League.

Japan had successfully defied the League. Collective security had been tested and it had failed to stop a determined aggressor – a message that was not likely to be lost on other potentially aggressive powers.

1

Appeasement and the Road to War

Source question practice

Source Ⓐ

Peace and future cannon fodder

PEACE AND FUTURE CANNON FODDER

The Tiger: "Curious! I seem to hear a child weeping!"

This cartoon, published in the Daily Herald on 17 May 1919, predicted the consequences of the Treaty of Versailles with extraordinary accuracy. The cartoonist, Will Dyson, was an Australian who worked for the Daily Herald at this time.

It shows the allied leaders leaving the Paris Peace Conference. Clemenceau of France (nicknamed the Tiger) is saying, 'Curious, I seem to hear a child weeping.' The other figures represent President Wilson for the USA, Prime Minister Lloyd George for Britain and Prime Minister Orlando, the Italian representative.

Your knowledge and understanding of 'Appeasement and the Road to War' will be assessed through five source-based questions, one of which is likely to be based on an illustration or cartoon.

Here is a worked example of one type of question that you will encounter.

1   How useful is **Source A** as evidence that already by 1919 there were concerns about the effectiveness of the peace treaties?

In reaching a conclusion you should refer to:

○   the origin and possible purpose of the source
○   the content of the source
○   recalled knowledge.

▶

This SQA prompt reminds you what you have to do to answer the question correctly – don't ignore it!

A good answer might read as follows.

The cartoon is quite useful as evidence of the legacy of the Peace Treaties, although it presents a very negative view of what had been decided in Paris. It is a contemporary source, published in May 1919, but it shows a remarkable far-sightedness, because it anticipates that there would be another war in about twenty years. It is likely that the cartoonist wanted to draw attention to the potential problems created by the peacemakers.

The cartoon shows Georges Clemenceau, the French Prime Minister nicknamed 'the Tiger', listening to a weeping child. This child symbolises the generation of young men who will be old enough to fight in 1940, and at his feet lies a Peace Treaty – a reference to the Treaties currently being drawn up in Paris. The cartoonist seems to suggest that those who drew up the treaties have caused the child's grief.

The cartoonist was clearly critical of the Peace Treaties. Nowadays, many historians view the legacy of the peace treaties less harshly. The peacemakers tried hard to draw up a lasting settlement and many of the decisions that they took were sound. The League of Nations was established as part of the peace treaties and in 1919 most people were optimistic that it would be able to prevent war in the future. So it is clear that Will Dyson's cartoon provides a useful but one-sided comment on the legacy of the peace treaties.

British foreign policy and the roots of appeasement

Introduction

From the early 1920s until March 1939 Britain was committed to a policy of appeasement. Although historians have used the term to suggest different things at different times, appeasement is normally defined as the policy of seeking to remedy grievances through negotiations, and making concessions in order to reduce international tensions and avoid war.

The circumstances in which appeasement occurs can differ. When sensible and justified concessions are made by a stronger country to a weaker one, then the policy is usually regarded as a wise and sensible approach to avoiding war.

However, when concessions are made from a position of weakness – when giving way to the unreasonable and unjustified demands of a bullying aggressor seems to be the only way of avoiding war – then the policy of appeasement is open to criticism. In both cases, however, the process is correctly known as appeasement.

Why did Britain follow a policy of appeasement in the 1920s?

1. Many people believed that the Treaty of Versailles treated Germany too harshly

The policy of appeasement can be traced back to British reaction to the way in which Germany was treated by the terms of the Treaty of Versailles.

In 1919, David Lloyd George, the British Prime Minister, disagreed with the French Prime Minister about the peace terms imposed on Germany. Privately, Lloyd George criticised those aspects of the treaty which would prove 'a constant source of irritation', especially those territorial terms which would leave ethnic Germans ruled by non-German governments. In April 1919, he wrote:

> *I cannot conceive any greater cause of future war than that the German people should be surrounded by a number of small states, many of them consisting of people who have never previously set up a stable government for themselves, but each of them containing large masses of Germans clamouring for reunion with their native land.*

Lloyd George lost the argument and, though the French made some concessions, the final terms were much harsher than many in Britain wanted. But from the start, people believed that the terms could be altered in the future. As one government minister wrote, once the treaty had been signed, there could be 'an appeasement, and by degrees readjustments and modifications can be introduced which will give Europe a prospect of stability'.

JM Keynes, a brilliant young economist who had been a member of the British delegation in Paris in 1919, added to the doubts about the Treaty of Versailles. In '*The economic consequences of the Peace*', published in 1919, he pointed out that the treaty did nothing to help restore the European economy, which had been devastated by the war. He argued that the reparations imposed on Germany would devastate European trade and lead to economic collapse. Although some historians believe that Keynes exaggerated the effects of reparations, his book helped to persuade people of the need for appeasement.

2. The recent war was so horrifying that it must never be repeated

World War One had affected almost every family in Britain. Those who had found themselves caught up in the fighting, and who had witnessed the slaughter, hoped that their sacrifice would be worthwhile and that Britain would indeed be the 'Land fit for heroes' promised by the government. War would play no part in that future. As one man wrote, shortly before he was killed in France:

> *Nothing but immeasurable improvements will ever justify all the waste and unfairness of this war – I only hope that those who are left will never, ever forget at what sacrifice those improvements have been won.*

After his death, this letter by Norman Chamberlain was published by his cousin, Neville. By 1937, Neville Chamberlain had become Prime Minister, and perhaps it is no coincidence that he would, in due course, become the man most associated with appeasement and the determination to do everything possible to avoid war.

With most ordinary people longing for peace, public opinion influenced British governments more than ever before. The Representation of the People Act of 1918 had extended the right to vote to all adult men, as well as many women over thirty, and governments now had to take the interests of the new electorate into consideration. The historian Martin Gilbert argues that 'Peace was the only policy the British people seemed willing to endorse. Fear of war dominated and oppressed the public mind'.

3. Britain could not afford high defence spending in the post-war world

By 1918, the war had been costing Britain £7m a day. The county's national debt was eleven times as large as it was in 1914, and the interest payments alone used up much of the government's income. After over four years of war-time production, many of Britain's industries were uncompetitive, while valuable overseas markets had been lost. As a result, the British economy was depressed throughout the 1920s, further increasing economic problems.

Given Britain's economic problems, defence expenditure was reduced drastically. In 1919 the government decide to base defence spending on the assumption that there would be no major war involving British forces in the next ten years. Defence spending was cut by more than a half in 1920 and then halved again over the next two years. In 1922, Britain accepted that the US Navy should be the same size as the British navy, and so gave up the claim that the Royal Navy should be the largest in the world. At the same time all five of the world's leading naval powers, including Britain, agreed that they would halt the construction of new ships for ten years.

Although Britain still clung to its role as a great power with a large empire around the world, it was clear that the country could no longer afford to be the policeman of the world. Appeasement was therefore an attractive way of avoiding conflict.

Appeasement in practice in the 1920s

Although the British public remained suspicious of Germany, it can be argued that British governments followed a policy of appeasement in the 1920s, since both the Conservative governments led by Bonar Law and Baldwin, and the Labour governments headed by Ramsey MacDonald, worked to reduce tensions between Germany and the rest of Europe.

When French troops occupied the Ruhr area of Germany in 1923, Britain opposed the French action, claiming that it increased German resentment. The following year Britain supported the American Dawes Plan, which

Source  2.1

A contemporary cartoon commenting favourably on the effects of the Dawes Plan

modified reparation payments and provided Germany with massive loans. The historian Frank McDonough has described the Dawes plan as 'the first major act of appeasement'.

The Locarno Agreements of 1925 marked a major breakthrough in the quest for peace. The British Foreign Secretary, Austen Chamberlain, played a crucial role in bringing together the French and German foreign ministers. Between them they hammered out a series of agreements which confirmed Germany's western frontiers as those established at Versailles, although there was no such confirmation of Germany's eastern frontiers. Most importantly, though, Locarno seemed to mark the beginning of a new period of cooperation, when all the major powers would be able to negotiate together and recognise each other's legitimate demands.

After Locarno, there were four years of greatly improved relations between Britain, France and Germany. Historians sometimes call this period 'the Locarno honeymoon'.

In 1926 Germany was admitted to the League of Nations and in 1927 ten thousand Allied troops stationed in the Rhineland were withdrawn. Finally, in 1929 the Young Committee further reduced reparation payments and at the same time Britain and Germany put pressure on France to accept that all the remaining troops should be withdrawn from the Rhineland. That happened in 1930, when the last French occupation troops were withdrawn from the Rhineland – five years earlier than was originally intended.

2

Source 2.2

A contemporary postcard, reflecting popular opinion in Germany. The rising sun of 1930 brings freedom to the Rhineland

Source 2.3

A photo from 1930, showing a class of children celebrating the withdrawal of the last French troops

For a short time at the end of the 1920s it had seemed that Europe was edging towards a more stable and peaceful age, and that the British policy of appeasement, in the sense of seeking to remedy grievances through negotiation, was working. However that optimism was shattered by the 1929 Wall Street Crash and its economic repercussions in Europe.

Activity

This chapter suggests three main reasons why Britain was prepared to appease Germany in the 1920s.

1 Which of these reasons do you consider was most influential among ordinary people?

2 Which do you consider was most influential in government circles?

In both cases, you should be able to justify your answer.

Source question practice

Source A

Our task is not to destroy but to build. Even a diminished Germany will still be the greatest state in Europe… A wise policy will treat Germany no longer as an enemy, but as a part of Europe… which for many a long year will need all our help and all our care to save it from ruin… For us the fundamental question is whether we desire a peace of appeasement or a peace of violence.

From the editorial of the *Manchester Guardian*, 10 May 1919. (The article was written as a comment on the German protests about the terms of the Draft Treaty, which had been handed to them three days earlier.)

1. To what extent does **Source A** explain the origins of appeasement in the 1920s?

Use the source and recalled knowledge.

This is typical of another type of question used in the Higher History exam. Here you are asked 'To what extent does the source explain…?' but there are other possible ways of asking much the same thing. For instance, you will come across questions which begin 'How fully does the source explain…', 'How far do you agree with the explanation given in the source…?' and 'How accurately does the source explain…?' These questions are very similar to the example given here. In each case, the 'prompt' written below the question will tell you to use the source and recalled knowledge.

A good answer to Question 1 might read something like the one below. Notice how the answer makes use of evidence from both the source and from recall to provide a balanced evaluation.

Source A provides a partial explanation of the origins of appeasement in the 1920s. Published in May 1919, this article provides us with an insight into one reaction to the proposed terms of the Treaty of Versailles.

The Manchester Guardian editorial appears to be critical of the severity of the terms of the Treaty and suggests that the peacemakers should be looking to the future, rather than punishing Germany for what had happened. The article goes on to suggest that Germany should be treated not as an enemy but as an important European country that will need support in the future if it is to avoid political and economic disaster. The editor states that Britain is faced with a choice of either appeasing Germany or facing further violence in the future, making it clear that in the editor's view appeasement is the only acceptable way forward.

This editorial reflects the views of a number of government ministers, as well as that of the economist JM Keynes, who argued that Germany had been treated too harshly. The Prime Minister Lloyd George was in favour of treating Germany more leniently and argued in favour of appeasing, or pacifying, Germany by making concessions, although he was unable to persuade the French to do this. In 'The Economic Consequences of the Peace', JM Keynes provided a sound economic argument in favour of appeasement when he claimed that there would be major economic problems in the future if Germany was crippled economically.

However, Source A does not provide a full explanation of the origins of appeasement in the 1920s. For most people the real roots of appeasement lay in their absolute determination to avoid another war at all costs, given the appalling slaughter of the war that had just ended. Britain faced huge social and economic problems at home and as a result defence spending was cut, making a policy of appeasement more attractive. So, even in the 1920s, appeasing Germany by trying to remove grievances had considerable appeal.

Since Source A does not mention the widespread rejection of war, or Britain's economic problems and the determination to cut defence spending, it provides only a partial explanation of the origins of appeasement. Nevertheless, it identifies an important argument used by those who wanted to appease Germany in the 1920s.

3 The rise of fascism

Introduction

Most people in Britain today are familiar with the word 'fascist' when used as a term of abuse. All too often it is simply used to describe beliefs or actions which – rightly or wrongly – are considered unacceptable. Originally, however, the words 'fascist' and 'fascism' had a much more specific meaning.

Fascism emerged in Italy immediately after World War One, although similar ideologies were evolving elsewhere. Fascism rejected democracy, believing that the existence of different political viewpoints weakened the state. It taught that the nation was more important than the individual, and that strong government with control over *all* social and economic activity was essential to national survival. Under a fascist government, national leadership would be entrusted to a single individual, who would command the loyalty of every citizen; all political opposition would be suppressed, and carefully controlled propaganda would be used to unite the people behind the image of the leader. As Mussolini himself put it, 'everything [is] in the State, nothing outside the State, nothing against the State'.

These ideas appealed to many different social classes in the aftermath of World War One. In particular, they seemed to offer an alternative to communism, at a time when democracy was faltering. By 1922 the first fascist government had been established in Italy by Benito Mussolini who became known as *Il Duce* – The Leader.

In Germany, Adolf Hitler was much impressed by what Mussolini had achieved, although it was not until the Great Depression blighted Germany after 1929 that he was able to match Mussolini's political success.

Both Mussolini and Hitler were committed to an expansionist foreign policy. Although their individual motives were different, both men believed that extending the frontiers of the state would demonstrate the energy and vitality of the nation. However historians do not agree about how far either man's foreign policy was determined by ideology and how far it was a pragmatic response to particular circumstances.

Source 3.1

Adolf Hitler and Mussolini shared many foreign policy goals

The foreign policy aims of Mussolini and Hitler

Italy, like Germany, was disappointed by the Paris Peace Settlement. Mussolini spoke of the national humiliation of his country's 'mutilated victory' in World War One, when Italy did not obtain all of the Habsburg, or Austrian, lands that it had coveted. Promising to rebuild the glories of the Roman Empire, Mussolini hoped to build up Italian influence around the Mediterranean, in the Balkans and in Africa. He referred to the Mediterranean as *mare nostrum* – 'our sea'. His stated aim was simple: 'I want to make Italy great, respected and feared.'

Likewise, Hitler also wanted to expand German influence but his targets lay in eastern Europe and Russia. Hitler and the Nazi Party's foreign policy aims in the 1920s were based on the Nazi Party's 25 Point Programme.

Although Hitler abandoned many of the points once in power, the first three remained central to Nazi ideology.

> 1. *We demand the union of all Germany in a Greater Germany based on the right of national self-determination.*
>
> 2. *We demand equality of rights for the German people in its dealings with other nations, and the destruction of the peace treaties of Versailles and Saint-Germain [The Treaty signed between Austria and the Allies in 1919].*
>
> 3. *We demand land and territory [colonies] to feed our people and to settle our surplus population.*

From the 25 Point Programme

These ideas were not new, nor were they unique to Hitler. In the early 1920s there were many right-wing groups opposed to the Treaty of Versailles – the shameful peace – and there had been calls for the unification of all Germans long before World War One from groups referred to as Pan-Germans. For many years, these Pan-Germans had also demanded *lebensraum* (living space) in Eastern Europe. They believed that if the German people were to thrive in the future they needed to be able to expand eastwards into areas occupied by the Slav peoples of eastern Europe.

During World War One, the Pan-Germans had argued in favour of the seizure of large areas of western Russia, which would then be settled by German farmers. When Russia was forced to surrender large areas of land to Germany by the terms of the treaty of Brest-Litovsk, it seemed as if their hopes had been fulfilled. The Treaty of Versailles, which took from Germany all of the land gained from Russia, was therefore a particular disappointment to those who believed in *lebensraum*. However, among the many extreme nationalist groups which thrived in post-war Germany, the dream of 'living space' in the east lived on.

In his earliest speeches, Hitler did not refer specifically to the demand for *lebensraum* in eastern Europe. But in his book *Mein Kampf*, published in two parts between 1924 and 1925, Hitler made the connection between the destruction of the Jews in Russia, whom he blamed for the Bolshevik seizure of power, and the acquisition of 'living space' in the east. From then on, Hitler associated his hatred of the Jews, as well as his belief that the Slavs of Eastern Europe were an 'inferior' people, with his demand for German expansion eastwards.

> "
> *The right to possess soil can become a duty if without extension of its soil a great nation seems doomed to destruction... And so we National Socialists take up where we broke off six hundred years ago. We stop the endless German movement to the south and west, and turn our gaze towards the lands of the east... If we speak of soil in Europe today, we can primarily have in mind only Russia and her vassal border states... The giant empire in the east is ripe for collapse. And the end of Jewish rule in Russia will also be the end of Russia as a state.*
>
> Mein Kampf, Vol. 2, quoted in Ian Kershaw, Hitler 1889–1936: Hubris, 1998

The other main strand in Hitler's statements about Nazi foreign policy in the later 1920s was his frequent attacks on communism, often called Bolshevism. In *Mein Kampf* he had written:

> The menace which Russia suffered under is one which perpetually hangs over Germany. Germany is the next great objective of Bolshevism. All our strength is needed to raise up our nation once more and rescue it from the embrace of the international python... The first essential is the expulsion of the Marxist poison from the body of our nation.

While much of Hitler's attention at this time focused on the activities of the German Communist Party, his desire to destroy the source of the international communist movement – the USSR – was also apparent. He talked of 'smashing' Bolshevik Russia, as well as the German Communist Party.

In the *Zweites Buch* (the Second Book), which Hitler dictated in 1928, but which was never published in Hitler's lifetime, he developed further his ideas about foreign policy. In particular, he argued that rearmament was essential, so that Germany could crush France and Russia, the two states which most threatened German domination of Europe. He identified Britain and Italy as potential allies, and speculated about the possibility of a contest for world domination between the USA and Europe.

Some historians have taken the ideas expressed in the *Zweites Buch* as a clear indication of Hitler's war plans for the future. Others, like Ian Kershaw, are more sceptical, and argue that the claims in the *Zweites Buch* about possible future conflict, with the USA in particular, simply reflect more general concerns in Germany in the 1920s.

Activity

1 Create a detailed spider diagram which identifies the key elements of Hitler's beliefs about German foreign policy. You should include:

- The revision of the Treaty of Versailles
- The expansion of German territory in the east
- The defeat of communism

2 Discuss your findings with a partner. How far do your diagrams agree?

Source question practice

Source A

The themes of Hitler's speeches (in the early 1920s) varied little: the contrast of Germany's strength in a glorious past with its current weakness and national humiliation – a sick state in the hands of traitors and cowards who had betrayed the Fatherland to its powerful enemies; …English and French intentions of destroying Germany, as shown in the Treaty of Versailles – the Peace of Shame', the instrument of Germany's slavery.

From Ian Kershaw, *Hitler 1889–1936: Hubris*, 1998.

Source B

If the National Socialist movement really wants to be consecrated by history with a great mission for our nation, …it must take up the struggle against the aimlessness and incompetence which have hitherto guided our German nation in the line of foreign affairs. Then, without consideration of 'traditions' and prejudices, it must find the courage to gather our people and their strength for an advance along the road that will lead this people from its present restricted living space to new land and soil, and hence also free it from the danger of vanishing from the earth or of serving others as a slave nation.

From *Mein Kampf*, Vol.2, 1926.

Source C

In his propaganda Hitler promised everything to everyone…It should be noted that many people in Germany at this time, particularly belonging to the younger generation, were Auslandsdeutsche (Germans born outside Germany): they had left their old homes in the new successor states where they felt, rightly or wrongly that they were unfairly treated, to seek their fortunes in Germany itself. Naturally they were delighted by the Nazi attitude which proposed to incorporate all Germans in Germany without saying how this could be done: this was one of the 25 points in the early Nationalist Socialist Programme.

From Elizabeth Wiskemann, *Europe of the Dictators*, 1966.

Sources A, B and **C** all refer to some aspect of Hitler's ideas about foreign policy. The question which follows is based on the eight-mark question, which is one of the five document questions in every paper. Since this is the first time that you have come across the 'three source' question, a possible answer has been provided.

1 How fully do **Sources A, B** and **C** explain Hitler's ideas about German foreign policy in the years before 1933?

*Use **Sources A, B** and **C** and recalled knowledge*

Although Hitler did not become Chancellor until January 1933, almost all of his ideas about German foreign policy can be traced back to what he said or wrote in the 1920s. Despite this, historians do not agree about Hitler's intentions: were these ideas a 'blueprint' for action or were they simply the ranting of a demagogue who wanted to achieve power?

In Source A, Kershaw analyses the content of Hitler's speeches in the early 1920s, when he contrasted Germany's glorious past with the humiliation of the Versailles settlement. Hitler was always an outspoken critic of the Treaty of Versailles, and of the 'November criminals' – those 'traitors and cowards who had betrayed the Fatherland' – who agreed to the armistice; it is therefore hardly surprising that the Nazi Party Programme of 1920 committed the newly formed party to overthrowing the Versailles Peace settlement.

These ideas were developed further in Mein Kampf. When he was in prison, Hitler wrote down his ideas about Germany's status in Europe and it was then that he started to demand not only the overthrow of the Versailles settlement but also German expansion eastwards. The 25 Point Programme of 1920 had already included the demand for land and territory in which to settle surplus population, but in Mein Kampf Hitler developed further the dangerous idea of acquiring 'living space' for Germans. As Source B shows, he believed that lebensraum was the only possible way of achieving security for the German people who otherwise faced the possibility of annihilation. Hitler also envisaged that the Slav nations of eastern Europe would provide Germany with important economic assets, which was not mentioned in the extract.

Source C illustrates Hitler's ability to identify popular policies and run with them. Many ethnic Germans, who were born outside Germany but who had recently returned to Germany, were delighted by his talk of creating a Gross Deutschland, unifying all ethnic Germans across Europe. As Source C emphasises, when Hitler spoke or wrote about such subjects, he was deliberately vague about how it would be achieved.

Taken together, the three sources go a long way to explaining Hitler's ideas about foreign policy in the years before 1933. However, they do not show the extent to which Hitler's ideas about foreign policy were indebted to the Pan-German movement, with its origins in the years before World War One; nor do they illustrate the extent to which anti-Semitism was inextricably linked to Hitler's expansionist ideas. There is no mention of his paranoid hatred of communism, and the way in which Hitler's fear of Bolshevism – which he associated with the Jews – influenced his ideas about Germany's foreign policy. Nor is there any direct reference to Hitler's determination to rearm Germany, even though this was specifically prohibited by the terms of the Treaty of Versailles.

What does emerge clearly from the three sources is the fact that during the years before 1933, Hitler's foreign policy aimed to appeal to large numbers of Germans, building on the resentment of Versailles and the desire to see Germany restored to its former alleged glory. Before 1933, Hitler's foreign policy was deliberately vague – in that way he would maximise his appeal – and it was only after 1933, when he was Chancellor, and later Fuhrer, of Germany, that his ideas gradually became incorporated in policy .

Hitler's foreign policy 1933–35

Introduction

Between 1930 and 1932 Germany had successfully challenged or defied the Treaty of Versailles. For example, at the World Disarmament Conference, organised by the League of Nations, Germany insisted that either other countries should reduce their armed forces to the same size as Germany's or, alternatively, Germany should be allowed to rearm until its armed forces were the same size as those of the other powers. Either way, Germany would achieve equality of armaments, and plans were made to increase the size of Germany's army by 1938.

Source 4.1

Contemporary illustration showing Germany surrounded by heavily armed neighbours. Note the size of the French armed forces, which angered every German government.

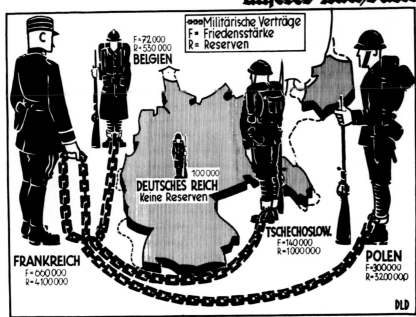

German rearmament gets underway

Within days of being sworn in as Chancellor, Hitler met with Germany's military leaders and made it clear that he wanted an immediate expansion of the army. At a Cabinet meeting on 8 February, he claimed that 'the next five years must be devoted to the defence capacity of the German people'. The following day, Hitler spoke at some length about the importance of rearmament, arguing that:

> *For Germany's rearmament, billions are necessary. The sum of 127 million Reich marks for aviation purposes was the minimum that one could consider at all. Germany's future depended exclusively and solely on rebuilding the armed forces. All other expenditure had to be subordinated to the task of rearmament... In any future clash between demands of the armed forces and demands for other purposes the interest of the armed forces had, whatever the circumstances, to take precedence.*
>
> From the minutes of the meeting, quoted by Kershaw, in Hitler 1889–1936: Hubris, 1998

German withdrawal from the Disarmament Conference and the League of Nations

By the time Hitler became Chancellor, the World Disarmament Conference in Geneva had reached deadlock. Hitler urged his ministers to be cautious in their demands, fearing that if they withdrew immediately from the Conference, then Britain and France might be so alarmed that they would intervene. However, it was increasingly clear that Britain and France did not agree about the way in which Germany should be treated, with Britain more inclined than the French to make some concessions. Speaking in the Reichstag, but knowing that all of Europe's statesmen would take note of what he said, Hitler emphasised Germany's weakness in armaments, when contrasted with the France's overwhelming superiority. He stated that Germany would renounce all weapons of aggression if other countries would do the same. He ended by threatening that, if the other powers insisted on discriminating against Germany, they clearly wanted to drive Germany out of the Disarmament Conference. Then, 'as a continually defamed people, it would be hard for us to stay in the League of Nations'.

The disarmament talks were postponed throughout the summer and only reconvened in October. At that point, Britain announced that it was taking

Source 4.2

This cartoon was published on 3 October 1933. The cartoonist David Low shows Hitler challenging Sir John Simon, Mussolini and Edouard Daladier, since they have failed to keep their League commitment to disarm.

"WELL – WHAT ARE YOU GOING TO DO ABOUT IT NOW?"

a tougher line on the issue of German rearmament than it had done previously. Hitler had the perfect excuse. Britain had slighted Germany and so the German government was justified in its decision to withdraw from both the Disarmament Conference and the League of Nations. On 14 October, the German government officially informed the Disarmament Conference of its decision.

The Non-Aggression Pact between Poland and Germany

German withdrawal from the League dealt a fatal blow to the idea of collective security. The Poles were quick to recognise this and, alarmed by the failure of the Western powers to act to stop Hitler from rearming Germany, they entered into negotiations with the German government. In January 1934 the two countries signed a ten-year Non-Aggression Pact.

Since France could no longer rely on Poland to put pressure on Germany's eastern frontier, the Non-Aggression Pact seriously weakened the alliance system that the French government had built up in eastern Europe (see Chapter 1). At the same time, Germany had broken out of the diplomatic

encirclement that the French had attempted to impose on it. For Hitler, this represented a clean break from the policies of previous German governments, which had shunned Poland since 1919, but it considerably strengthened his position in eastern Europe.

Intrigue and assassination in Austria

In July 1934 Austrian Nazis attempted to overthrow the Austrian government. Although the coup (attempted takeover) failed, the Austrian Chancellor, Engelbert Dollfuss, was assassinated. It is still not clear how accurate a knowledge Hitler had of the Austrian Nazis' plans, although he had undoubtedly encouraged them to make life difficult for Dollfuss in the preceding months.

The whole incident proved an embarrassment for Hitler, because he could not risk Italian involvement and Mussolini had already made it clear that he would intervene to prevent Germany meddling in Austrian affairs. When news of the attempted coup reached Rome, Mussolini moved troops to the Brenner frontier between Italy and Austria and Hitler was forced to publicly disassociate himself from what had happened. In mid-1934, Hitler clearly still had to proceed cautiously and could not risk angering a major European power.

The Saar plebiscite

In January 1935, Hitler's policies received a great propaganda boost when the people of the Saarland voted overwhelmingly to rejoin Germany. In 1919 the Saar had been transferred to France for fifteen years, with the promise that at the end of that time, there would be a plebiscite to determine what the people of the region wanted in the future. Of the 500,000 voters in the Saar, almost 91 per cent voted in favour of reunification with Germany. This result was particularly pleasing for Hitler, since over two-thirds of those who had previously voted for left-wing parties now demonstrated their support for Hitler's policies by voting in favour of rejoining Germany. Once again, Hitler took the opportunity to reassure the world of his peaceful intentions. In an interview with the *Daily Mail*, he stated that 'Germany will never of its own accord break the peace'.

The continuing story of German rearmament

On 1 March 1935 the Saar formally became part of Germany again. Hitler knew that the advantage temporarily lay with him and that he must seize the opportunity his triumph had presented. Within days Goering announced the existence of a German air force – which was, of course, specifically banned by the Treaty of Versailles. Six days later, Hitler addressed foreign ambassadors to inform them that he was about to announce the existence of a greatly enlarged army consisting of 36 divisions. The Treaty of Versailles permitted a total of ten. Conscription would be introduced to bring the army up to size. Again, this contravened the terms of the Treaty of Versailles.

That day special newspapers appeared announcing 'the first great measure to liquidate Versailles', while delighted crowds celebrated outside Hitler's headquarters, the Reich Chancellery. The following day, a Sunday, Hitler addressed the Reichstag. A magnificent military display followed the formal declaration of conscription and Hitler's plans for the German army.

Source 4.3

A parade during the Nazi Party Rally at Nuremberg, 1933

The Stresa Front

The news of German rearmament aroused the other European powers and brought them together temporarily. In April, the British Prime Minister, Ramsay MacDonald, Mussolini and Pierre Laval, the French Foreign Minister, met at Stresa in Italy to work out a common response to developments in Germany. The short-lived alliance between the three countries became known as the 'Stresa Front'.

The three countries confirmed their commitment to the Locarno Treaties, and declared that the independence of Austria 'would continue to inspire their common policy'. They also agreed they would resist any future attempt by the Germans to change the Treaty of Versailles.

For a short while it seemed possible that the Stresa Front countries would stand together against Hitler. But within less than a month, France had concluded a Mutual Assistance Pact with the Soviet Union, which alarmed its Stresa Front partners, since it threatened to bring communist influences into western Europe. In June, Britain struck the Stresa Front a further damaging blow by signing an agreement with Germany accepting German naval expansion, without consulting either France or Italy. When Mussolini invaded Abyssinia in October, the Stresa Front was finally destroyed.

The Anglo–German Naval Agreement

Immediately after the announcement that conscription was to be reintroduced in Germany, Britain sent a formal note of protest. At the same time, however, a meeting between Hitler and Sir John Simon, the British Foreign Secretary, was suggested.

This meeting took place on 25 March, with Anthony Eden, then Under-Secretary for Foreign Affairs, accompanying Simon. Hitler asserted Germany's right to equal treatment as far as the size of its armed forces were concerned, and demanded that the German navy should equal 35 per cent of the total strength of the British navy. This was an astonishing move, but it was obvious that Hitler was not in the mood to negotiate.

Nevertheless, Germany's position remained vulnerable and there was still a possibility that the powers might act to stop Hitler. As a result, he planned another highly publicised speech, in which he would protest his peaceful intentions. On 21 May, he claimed that 'the German Reich and, in particular, the present German Government, have no other wish than to live on friendly and peaceable terms with all neighbouring States… Germany needs peace and wants peace… Germany has neither the intention nor the wish to annex or incorporate Austria'. Much of the speech, though, was intended to persuade Britain to enter into negotiations relating to relative naval strengths. It was successful and, within a few days, Britain and Germany entered into naval talks along the precise lines suggested by Hitler in March.

Ribbentrop opened the negotiations for Germany by demanding the 35 per cent ratio, exactly as Hitler had suggested in March. He stated that this was 'not simply a demand put forward by the German side but the final decision by the German Chancellor'. Despite these crude negotiating tactics, it was swiftly apparent that the British would accept the terms. Ribbentrop's bullying technique had worked.

On 18 June, the Anglo–German naval agreement was finalised. It was agreed that Germany could build a navy that was 35 per cent of the size of the British navy, while its submarine fleet could equal Britain's. The Versailles restrictions on the German navy had been completely set aside.

To the French it seemed that Britain had shown no regard for its international commitments; to the British it seemed preferable to negotiate and make concessions, thereby retaining some control over the nature and extent of German rearmament. The British government had again shown its preference for appeasement, rather than confrontation.

Assessment of Hitler's foreign policy 1933–35

In just over two years, Nazi Germany had successfully defied the strict limitations that the Treaty of Versailles placed on the German armed forces. By the end of 1935 rearmament was well under way and major building programmes were being planned for both the German air force and the German navy. To reach this point, Hitler had employed a number of different tactics, including:

- diplomatic bullying of other European powers
- exposing the injustices of the Versailles settlement
- emphasising his allegedly peaceful intentions
- winning the support of large numbers of Germans.

Hitler had, however, acted more cautiously than he would do in the second half of the decade. He knew that it was vital to consolidate the position of his regime within Germany, and this had meant concentrating on domestic, rather than foreign affairs. In fact, it is clear that many of the foreign policy statements issued during Hitler's first year in power were prepared by the German Foreign Office, with little input from Hitler. He was also wary of the reaction that he might provoke abroad, for he knew that Germany was not yet in a position to resist foreign intervention, should the other European powers decide to act. Although the Stresa Front was short-lived, Germany was dangerously isolated during the summer of 1935, and Hitler could not afford to drive his potential enemies closer together. Instead he was determined to follow a policy which would aim to convince the British, in particular, of the reasonableness of his demands.

Was Hitler's foreign policy driven by a master plan drawn up before he became Chancellor?

For the last sixty years, historians have debated whether Hitler was fulfilling a planned course of action which would lead to a European war. Immediately after 1945, it seemed very plausible to claim that everything that Hitler did was part of just such a master plan. According to this view, Hitler's aims were set out in the 25 Point Programme, and then expanded

in *Mein Kampf* and the *Zweites Buch*. Once Hitler had achieved power, he set about rearming Germany, so that he was in a position to defy the other European powers and implement his expansionist policy. The Hossbach Memorandum (see Chapter 9) provided later proof of his intent.

In the 1960s, AJP Taylor, an historian who enjoyed provoking debate, challenged this view. In *The Origins of the Second World War* (1961), Taylor argued that Hitler, like other German leaders before him, was striving to make Germany the greatest power in Europe, but that he had no master plan. Instead, he seized every opportunity that was presented to him. In other words, Hitler was an opportunist, and the appeasers played into his hand.

Since then, the debate has moved on but it has been dominated by versions of these two different views. On the one hand, there are those historians who believe that Hitler was implementing a 'programme', which would lead to German domination in Europe, or possibly in the entire world. On the other hand, there are historians who do not accept the 'programme' argument and who maintain that Hitler did not decide on foreign policy on his own. They point to the many other groups in Germany with their own agendas, such as the army, the German Foreign Office, industrialists seeking new resources and markets and ordinary Nazi Party members calling for action. All of these, together with the mounting economic crisis, created pressures within German society that helped shape Hitler's foreign policy.

Activity

Between 1933 and 1935, Hitler's foreign policy was largely concerned with challenging the Treaty of Versailles.

1 Make a list of the ways in which Hitler had challenged the Versailles settlement.

2 Which of these do you consider to have been the most important for the future? Give reasons for your answer.

3 Explain the significance of:

   (a) the Non-Aggression Pact with Poland
   (b) the Stresa Front
   (c) the Anglo–German Naval Agreement

4 What evidence can you find to support the view that Hitler had a master plan for achieving European domination? What evidence is there that suggests that this was not the case? Why do you think that historians still disagree about this issue?

Source question practice

Source A

My Struggle (Mein Kampf) has been seen by some historians as a kind of blueprint for Hitler's later actions, a dangerous and devilish book that was unfortunately ignored by those who should have known better. It was nothing of the kind… Hitler's beliefs were clearly laid out in My Struggle, for all to see who wished to. No one familiar with the text could have emerged from reading it with the view that all Hitler wanted was the revision of the Treaty of Versailles, the restoration of the German borders of 1914 or the self-determination of German-speaking minorities in Central Europe. Nor could anyone have doubted the visceral, fanatical, indeed murderous qualities of his anti-Semitism. But beliefs and intentions are not the same as blueprints and plans.

From Richard Evans, *The Coming of the Third Reich*, 2003.

Source B

Other historians, especially those of the 'Programme School'… argue on the strength of Mein Kampf and Hitler's Second Book that he had a definite programme. First of all he planned to defeat France and Russia, and then, after building up a large navy, make a determined bid for world power, even if it involved war against both Britain and the USA.

From David Williamson, *War and Peace: International Relations*, 1919–39, 2003.

Source C

The first and indispensable step was for Germany to rearm. Until he had the backing of military power for his diplomacy, Hitler's foreign policy was bound to be restricted in its scope. This period during which the German Armed Forces were being expanded and re-equipped was one of considerable danger. Until rearmament reached a certain stage Germany was highly vulnerable to any preventative action which France or the other Powers might take… The overriding objective of German foreign policy, therefore, for the first years of Hitler's regime, was to avoid such action, and thus to secure the time and freedom to rebuild Germany's military power.

From Alan Bullock, *Hitler: A Study in Tyranny*, 1952.

1 Compare the views given in **Sources A** and **B** about the nature of Hitler's foreign policy.

Compare the sources overall and in detail.

There is one source comparison question in every Higher History exam, in Paper 2. In this example, the two sources are secondary sources but you could be asked to compare two primary sources, or a primary source and a secondary source.

▶

When comparing two sources, you are asked to compare them overall, and in detail. You should aim to start with a general statement about the similarities or differences between the two sources. Then you should compare the two sources directly, point by point. Since the sources in this example are relatively short, there are not very many different points of comparison; even so, the answer moves from the generalisation to some specific, detailed comparisons. Make sure that you finish your answer with a concluding sentence.

Sources A and B represent very different views about the nature of Hitler's foreign policy. They outline two opposing views in the ongoing debate about whether or not Hitler had a master plan which, right from the outset, he intended to implement.

In Source A, the historian Richard Evans makes it clear that he rejects the view that Hitler had a definite blueprint, or plan of action, for the conduct of German foreign policy, whereas Source B puts forward the argument used by the so-called 'programme' school of historians who believe that Hitler did have a master plan which he intended to implement.

The two sources both mention Mein Kampf but they interpret its significance very differently. Source A accepts that Mein Kampf reflects Hitler's fanatical beliefs but Richard Evans points out that beliefs are not the same as a plan of action, or blueprint, whereas Source B states that historians of the so-called 'Programme School' believe that Hitler was indeed establishing a definite plan of action when he wrote Mein Kampf and the Second Book.

Source A then goes on to mention some of Hitler's hopes for the future: he wanted a revision of the terms of the hated Versailles 'diktat' and he longed for the restoration of Germany's 1914 frontiers. Above all, he wanted ethnic Germans, living outside the Reich, to have the right to chose their own form of government – which Hitler doubtless believed would lead to their inclusion in a Greater Germany. But, according to Evans, these were just aspirations, not clear-cut plans. Source B also mentions specific aspects of Hitler's foreign policy but interprets their significance very differently. Hitler's demands are presented as deliberately contrived stepping stones on the route to world domination. From the outset, he planned war with France and the USSR, so that he could defeat them; after that, he would make a bid for world domination, even if this necessitated war with Britain and the USA.

Although the two extracts are brief, they provide a good summary of two very different views about the nature of Hitler's foreign policy.

2 How far do you accept the analysis of Hitler's foreign policy priorities given in **Source C**?

5 Appeasement in the 1930s

Introduction

With their governments struggling to cope with domestic problems, both Britain and France lacked the determination and economic resources to challenge developments in Germany. As a result, both countries sought to avoid conflict and opted for compromise and negotiation which resulted in appeasement.

French policy in the 1930s

By the early 1930s, French society was deeply divided between left-wing and right-wing views. Public opinion was largely indifferent to what was happening outside France and successive governments failed to win support for a more interventionist approach. One recent historian has claimed that the French people and their leaders suffered a collective 'crisis of confidence' in the 1930s which left them unable to act. According to Anthony Adamthwaite, 'If rulers and ruled had possessed the courage to say *merde* to Hitler before 1939 the story would have had a different ending.'

As the Nazi threat became more apparent, the French relied heavily on their alliances with east European countries, but this policy was seriously undermined by the Polish–German Non-Aggression Pact. After January 1934, the French government tried to ensure

Source 5.1

After 1935, French right-wing propaganda played on the fear of a German attack from the air. This poster states: 'Look what awaits us if the Popular Front disarms France!'

VOILA CE QUI NOUS ATTEND DEMAIN, SI LE **FRONT COMMUN** DÉSARME LA FRANCE !

France's security by negotiating new agreements with other European countries. In January 1935, France and Italy agreed to act together if Germany should rearm or threaten Austrian independence. In April, the Stresa Front appeared to cement that friendship, and talks, this time about possible joint military action, followed in the summer.

The French also opened negotiations with the USSR, and when Germany announced the reintroduction of conscription in March 1935 French efforts to reach agreement with the Soviets intensified. In May the Franco–Soviet Pact was agreed, although it was not ratified by the French Parliament until February of the following year.

Although France still had the largest army in Europe in 1930, the experience of World War One left many determined to avoid war if possible. As a result, French military thinking focused increasingly on defensive strategies. After 1930, the construction of the Maginot Line proceeded apace. The Maginot Line was a huge network of fortifications along the French–German border, most of it underground so as to avoid French soldiers ever again having to face the horrors of the trench warfare of the Great War. However this line of defences not only absorbed most of France's military spending, it also created a static, defensive mentality and many historians believe that this lulled France into a false sense of security.

Factors affecting British Foreign policy 1933–37

By the 1930s there were additional reasons why British governments were prepared to appease Hitler.

Widespread hostility to war

There was a growing body of evidence that the British people were opposed to war.

In October 1933, a by-election took place in the London constituency of Fulham East. During the campaign the Labour Party candidate promised to support immediate general disarmament. On polling day he overturned a large Conservative majority to win the seat by 5,000 votes. At the time it was believed that this astonishing result reflected widespread pacifism, although nowadays it is thought that issues relating to unemployment and housing played an important part.

Stanley Baldwin was certainly influenced by the result. Three years later, as Prime Minister, he had this to say, when Churchill attacked him for his failure to rearm:

> *You will remember at that time [1932-3] the Disarmament Conference was sitting in Geneva. You will remember that at that time there was probably a stronger pacifist feeling running through this country than at any time since the war. I asked myself what chance was there, when that feeling that was given expression to in Fulham was common throughout the country, what chance was there, within the next year or two, of that feeling being so changed that the country would give a mandate for rearmament?*
>
> Stanley Baldwin in the House of Commons, 12 November 1936

In 1933, the Co-operative Women's Guild produced the first white poppies to be worn on Armistice Day. The Guild stressed that the white poppy was not intended as an insult to those who died in the First World War – a war in which many of the women lost husbands, brothers, sons and lovers. They argued that the world was drifting back to war and this feeling was picked up by the Peace Pledge Union.

In 1934, Dick Sheppard, a pacifist clergyman, wrote to the Manchester Guardian and other newspapers inviting men to send him a postcard promising to 'renounce war and never again support another'. He received 2,500 replies within two days and within a few weeks some 30,000 had made this pledge. The Peace Pledge Union, as it became known, had over 100,000 members by 1936, including such well-known figures as the poet Siegfried Sassoon, the philosopher Bertrand Russell, the author Aldous Huxley and George Lansbury, the leader of the Labour opposition in the House of Commons until 1935. The PPU had its own newspaper, with a circulation of 22,000.

In 1933 a very different group of young men had demonstrated their support for pacifism. The Oxford University Union had debated the motion: 'This House will under no circumstances fight for King and Country' and the motion had been carried by 275 votes to 153.

In 1918 the League of Nations Union had been established to win

Source 5.2

Posters outside the Peace Pledge Union Peace Centre in Birmingham, 1939

support for the League and its commitment to collective security and disarmament. In 1935 it organised a Peace Ballot, when voters were asked to vote on various issues concerning peace. Over 11 million people participated, revealing overwhelming support for collective security, and for the League of Nations and disarmament. A further survey in July 1937 revealed that at that time 71 per cent of the British people thought that supporting the League of Nations was the best way of keeping the peace.

Fear of modern warfare

In the 1930s, memories of World War One remained very powerful. Books like *Goodbye to All That* by Robert Graves (published in 1929), and the 1930 award-winning film *All Quiet on the Western Front* intensified the widespread rejection of war.

There were new threats as well, which made the prospect of war seem even more unacceptable. By the 1930s, the potential of air power in war was fully recognised. The development of the bomber had changed the nature of warfare forever. The great fear was that bombers would be used against civilian populations, as well as strategic and industrial targets. As Stanley Baldwin told the House of Commons in 1932, 'I think it is as well… for the man in the street to realise that no power on earth can protect him from being bombed. Whatever people may tell him, the

Source 5.3

Bombed-out buildings of Guernica, destroyed in the Spanish Civil War

bomber will always get through'. The reality of bombing raids in Abyssinia (see Chapter 6) and Guernica (see Chapter 8), combined with the graphic depiction of the fictitious bombing of London in the 1936 science fiction film, *Things to Come*, which predicted a devastating war in 1940, left a lasting impression of horror which few politicians were prepared to ignore.

The threat of communism

For many Conservative politicians and for many ordinary British people as well, the threat of communism was the most pressing problem of the 1930s. 'As a result, Germany was seen as the best hope of preventing the spread of Bolshevism. However objectionable it might be in some respects, Nazism was preferable to Communism' (Ian Kershaw, *Making Friends With Hitler*, 2004). Lord Rothermere, the wealthy newspaper proprietor, expressed a popular right-wing view when he wrote in a *Daily Mail* editorial in November 1933 that 'sturdy young Nazis' were 'Europe's guardians against the Communist danger'.

Failure to recognise Hitler as a threat

Before 1930, few people had taken much notice of Adolf Hitler. The British press had been dismissive of the man whom the *Observer* described as 'a ranting fool', and it was only with Hitler's rapid rise to power during 1932–33 that media coverage brought Hitler to the attention of the British public. Conservative newspapers, including *The Times*, the *Daily Telegraph* and the *Daily Mail*, were not unduly concerned about developments in Germany. Even after the Night of the Long Knives massacre when Hitler ordered the murder of the leadership of the SA, *The Times* came to the conclusion that 'during the next few years there is more reason to be afraid for Germany than to be afraid of Germany'. Even the left-wing *Daily Herald*, the paper with the largest circulation in Britain, at first failed to recognise the scale of the Nazi threat, although it would later be an outspoken critic of appeasement. Only *The Manchester Guardian* was consistently hostile.

During the brief period between 1933 and 1935, when Germany remained militarily weak, the British government was unable to decide what to make of Hitler. By the time that the Cabinet came to terms with what Churchill had been claiming since 1933 – that Nazi Germany posed a threat to European security, and that Hitler was aiming to make Germany the dominant power in Europe – there was little that Britain could do.

Hitler's demands were seen as justified

Hitler was committed to a revision of the Treaty of Versailles and British politicians had been critical of aspects of the Treaty for a long time. Between 1933 and 1936 there was a widespread acceptance that Hitler's

demands relating to the Treaty of Versailles were justified. In particular, people recognised that the almost complete disarmament of Germany had left it vulnerable to attack. At the same time, Hitler's skilful use of propaganda succeeded in convincing people that he was looking to restore Germany to its rightful position in Europe, but that his ambitions did not threaten European peace.

Britain was not ready to fight

Britain had cut defence spending drastically after World War One. Successive governments supported disarmament, believing it would reduce the likelihood of war and make further defence spending cuts possible. By 1932, however, it was clear that the world was changing, and that, although the Disarmament Conference was finally underway, it was unlikely to succeed.

In 1932 the '10 year rule', introduced in 1919, was suspended: policy would no longer be based on the assumption that there would be no major war in the next ten years. The following year, Prime Minister Ramsey MacDonald set up the Defence Requirements Committee to make recommendations about future defence spending. But Britain could ill-afford to increase spending on the armed forces in 1934, and it was not until 1937 that defence spending increased dramatically.

Because the country was not prepared for war, and because Britain's interests in the Far East and Mediterranean were also threatened, the Chiefs of Staff urged the government to avoid war. Others were arguing much the same thing: Britain needed time to rearm and appeasement was a way of gaining time.

Collective security did not appear to work

Although the vast majority of people wanted the League of Nations to work, it did not seem to be able to provide solutions to problems when they arose. The League's weaknesses had been exposed when Japan occupied Manchuria, and it had failed to achieve one of its key aims: international disarmament. The Italian invasion of Abyssinia (see Chapter 6) had destroyed what little remaining credibility the League still had. After 1936, it was clear that the League of Nations was not likely to provide a solution to international problems.

The Dominions were not prepared to support Britain

In World War One Britain had relied heavily on support from its Empire. The decision to involve even the most self-governing parts of the Empire – Canada, Australia, New Zealand and South Africa – had been taken in London. By 1931, however, these Dominions had achieved complete

independence from Britain in foreign affairs. This meant that they would be free to decide whether they wanted to support Britain in any future war.

At the 1937 Imperial Prime Ministers Conference, the question of defence was high on the agenda. The Prime Ministers of Canada, Australia and South Africa made it clear that they favoured a policy of appeasement and that they would not necessarily support Britain if the country went to war. Baldwin resigned as Prime Minister at the beginning of the Conference and Chamberlain must have been influenced by these views.

The USA was following a policy of isolation and strict neutrality

Allied victory in 1918 owed a great deal to the United States' entry into the war the previous year. After 1918, however, the mood in America changed. In 1920 the Republican candidate won the presidential election and promised America a 'return to normalcy'. In terms of foreign affairs, 'normalcy' meant not getting involved in European affairs. Although US governments supported measures that promoted disarmament (observers attended the Disarmament Conference) or the renunciation of war (the US and France were responsible for the Kellogg–Briand Pact of 1928 which invited countries to renounce war as an instrument of national policy), for the next twenty years, the USA remained largely isolated from European affairs, and did not commit itself to any alliances.

The Great Depression heightened US withdrawal from European affairs. In 1935, the US government passed the Neutrality Act which was designed to keep America out of a possible European war by banning the sale of armaments to belligerents . The Act was subsequently extended to include Civil wars, and to ban loans to belligerents.

The message to Europe was clear: there should be no expectation of help from the USA.

Changing views of Nazi Germany

Attitudes towards Germany changed considerably between 1933 and 1937, and as a result so did attitudes towards appeasement. Frank McDonough argues that by 1936 'Nazi Germany was no longer viewed as a weak and defeated power but as a menacing threat'; even so, Baldwin's government still clung to the idea of trying to find ways of reaching some sort of agreement with Nazi Germany which would include all of the European countries affected by developments in Germany.

Early in 1937, the Foreign Secretary Anthony Eden informed ministerial colleagues that the prospects for a general settlement with Germany were 'very small'. Yet ministers felt that the best way forward was to continue to follow a policy of conciliation and compromise. By this time, however,

Britain was clearly appeasing Germany from a position of weakness, rather than strength.

Opposing appeasement

Within the Conservative Party there were a few outspoken opponents of appeasement in the years 1933–37. The most notable among them was Winston Churchill, who argued in favour of rearmament from 1933 onwards.

The position of the Labour Party was ambiguous. Although they had supported the appeasement of justified German grievances before 1933, they opposed the appeasement of Nazi Germany because they believed that the regime was inherently evil. At the same time, they consistently opposed increased spending on rearmament, which they believed made war more likely, and remained firmly committed to the principles of the League of Nations. When collective security appeared to be failing, a minority within the party were highly critical of the League, with some going so far as to advocate an alliance with the Soviet Union.

The Spanish Civil War marked a turning point for Labour. As the party became increasingly critical of appeasement, so Labour's attitude towards rearmament slowly began to change and by the spring of 1938 the Labour leader, Clement Attlee, was criticising the government for not spending enough on air defences.

By the mid-1930s there were only about 20 Liberal MPs in the House of Commons, led by Sir John Simon. Like the Labour Party, they were very committed to the League of Nations and collective security. The Spanish Civil War brought about a gradual change in Liberal thinking and by 1938, like Labour, they were increasingly critical of Chamberlain's policies.

Who's who? – the appeasers

Lord Lothian: A leading Liberal in the House of Lords. An advocate of appeasement until 1939, Lothian believed that personal contact with leading Nazis would lead to greater understanding and defuse the international situation. He often presented Hitler's views in a very favourable light in the British press.

Lord Halifax: Appointed Foreign Secretary in February 1938 when Eden resigned. The previous November, Chamberlain had sent Halifax to Berlin to meet with Hitler. Halifax had strongly anti-communist views and told Hitler that he approved of the way the Nazis were dealing with communists in Germany.

Henry 'Chips' Channon: An American by birth, Channon was a junior Minister in Chamberlain's government in 1938. He was a committed

supporter of General Franco in Spain and favoured appeasement, partly because he hoped Hitler might be persuaded to attack the Soviet Union.

Samuel Hoare (Lord Templewood): Hoare was Foreign Secretary in 1935, until he was forced to resign when news of the proposed Hoare–Laval Pact was leaked. His willingness to appease Mussolini was rejected by the rest of the Cabinet. His support for appeasement appealed to Chamberlain, who brought him back into the government.

Sir Nevile Henderson: British Ambassador in Berlin between 1937 and 1939. Henderson showed considerable sympathy for the Nazis, so that his critics nicknamed him 'Our Nazi ambassador in Berlin'. In 1940 he published his memoirs, in an attempt to justify his actions as ambassador.

Lord Londonderry: Air Minister from 1931 until 1935, when he was sacked. In the second half of the 1930s, Londonderry worked to achieve a closer understanding by pursuing friendship with the Nazis at all costs. His pro-Nazi sympathies lost him support in Britain.

Who's who? – the anti-appeasers

Winston Churchill: A backbench Conservative MP from 1929–1940, Churchill was a leading advocate of rearmament and an outspoken critic of appeasement. He described the Munich agreement as 'the blackest page in British history'.

Anthony Eden and the 'Glamour Boys': Eden resigned from the post of Foreign Secretary in February 1938 because he could no longer accept Chamberlain's policy of appeasement. A group of about 25 MPs supported Eden, including Harold Macmillan.

Sir Robert (Bob) Boothby: A Conservative MP who joined Churchill and Leo Amery in demanding an increase in defence spending. From 1933 onwards, he was outspoken about Hitler and the threat that he posed. Looking back on the 1930s, he wrote in his memoirs:

> *The Conservative Party was rotten at the core. The only thing they cared about was their property and their cash. The only thing they feared was that one day those nasty Communists would come and take it.*
>
> *The Labour and Liberal Parties were no better. With the exception of Hugh Dalton… they made violent, pacifist speeches; and voted steadily against the miserable Defence Estimates for the years 1935, 1936, 1937 and 1938.*
>
> *Boothby in 1978 (Spartacus)*

Duff Cooper: Secretary of State for War 1935–37 and then First Lord of the Admiralty in Chamberlain's government until he resigned in protest at the Munich agreement.

Vernon Bartlett: a journalist who was severely critical of Chamberlain's policy of appeasement. He became an MP in November 1938 when he stood for election as an anti-Chamberlain candidate.

David Low: A cartoonist from New Zealand whose cartoons appeared in the Evening Standard throughout the 1930s. Low's cartoons often commented very critically on the decisions of leading politicians at home and abroad.

Activity

In this chapter, you have read about a range of reasons why people supported appeasement between 1933 and 1937. While it is important to remember that people are individuals, and that they do not all think alike, it is possible to generalise about why groups of people tended to support particular points of view.

Working with a partner:

1 Decide whether you think each person mentioned below was likely to have supported appeasement.

2 For each of the people you believe would have supported appeasement, decide which pro-appeasement arguments he or she would have used.

   ○ The widow of a soldier killed in action in World War One

   ○ A life-long Labour Party member

   ○ A professional diplomat

   ○ An army officer

   ○ A member of Stanley Baldwin's Cabinet

   ○ A backbench Conservative MP, friendly with Bob Boothby

3 Compare your decisions with others in your class.

Source question practice

Source A

There is now no prospect of a disarmament Convention and not even of a legalisation of Germany's illegal armaments. There is little inducement therefore to keep up appearances on either side. Besides, the continuing growth of Germany's armaments makes both secrecy [on Germany's part] and feigned ignorance [on Britain's part] increasingly difficult.

We have therefore been considering whether it is worthwhile maintaining our previous attitude; and whether the Berlin Embassy should not from now onwards in their intercourse with German Ministers and officials, proceed... on the assumption that each side recognises Germany's violation and Germany's intention to violate Part V of the Treaty of Versailles.

From a Foreign Office Memorandum to the Berlin Embassy, October 1934.

Source B

Vansittart [Permanent Under-Secretary at the Foreign Office] firmly believed in the reports of Hitler's aggressive plans; he was certain the only method of blocking them was by British rearmament, and that as British rearmament would take years to complete, the need was to gain time and strengthen the allied front... Once convinced... I threw all the influence that I possessed into the double campaign for more arms and more time... Vansittart's refrain never ceased to ring in my head: 'We are terribly weak. We must gain time for becoming stronger. Only military strength will stop Hitler, and at present we do not possess it'.

From Viscount Templewood, *Nine Troubled Years*, 1954. Formerly Sir Samuel Hoare, the author was Foreign Secretary in 1935.

Source C

When I first went to Berlin, I thought it was unjust and impolitic to condemn a whole system because of certain of its more obvious vices. Moreover, I believed that there was no real prospect of stability either in Germany or in Europe generally until the grievances arising out of the Treaty of Versailles – which had created Hitler – had been rectified as far as the Germans were concerned. This done, I trusted that Hitler and the reasons for his existence and the methods of his regime would disappear. But in the meantime I thought that the right policy was to carry conciliation to its utmost point.

From Sir Nevile Henderson: *Failure of a Mission*, 1940.

Source D

It will be seen that our Navy, Military and Air Force... are still far from sufficient to meet our defence commitments, which now extend from Western Europe, through the Mediterranean to the Far East. We cannot foresee the time when our defence forces will be strong enough to safeguard our territory, trade and vital interests against Germany, Italy and Japan simultaneously. We cannot therefore exaggerate the importance from the point of view of Imperial Defence, of any political action that can be taken to reduce the numbers of our potential enemies and to gain the support of political allies.

From a report prepared by the Chiefs of Staff Committee 1937.

1 How useful is **Source A** as evidence of British attitudes towards German rearmament in the 1930s?

2 How far do **Sources B, C** and **D** explain why successive British National Governments were prepared to appease Nazi Germany in the years 1933–37?

Abyssinia and the failure of collective security

Introduction

By early 1935 it was clear that Mussolini intended to extend the Italian Empire in Africa by conquering Abyssinia (present day Ethiopia).

The Invasion of Abyssinia

In early October, Italian troops started to invade. The League of Nations condemned Italy as an agressor. However, in the following months it became clear that the League was powerless to stop a determined agressor and collective security was seen to have failed.

In January 1935, the French Foreign Minister, Pierre Laval, visited Rome. Minor differences between the two countries were settled and the mood was reasonably friendly. Mussolini was encouraged, but to make certain that public opinion in France was also favourable, the French press was bribed to present Italy in a positive light.

At the same time, Italy was sounding out possible British reactions to an invasion of Abyssinia. It is likely that Mussolini was influenced by Britain's apparent willingness to appease Germany and that he believed that Britain would be prepared to negotiate with Italy over the future of Abyssinia. In January, the Italian ambassador in London, Dino Grandi, discussed Abyssinia with the British Foreign Secretary, although he did not reveal all of Mussolini's plans. 'Their policy is as hard to pin down as their fog', Grandi wrote back to Mussolini.

In April that year the meeting at Stresa (see Chapter 4) seems to have convinced Mussolini that neither France not Britain would stand in his way, and that he would be able to intervene in North Africa without losing their friendship.

On 3 October, Italian troops started their invasion of Abyssinia, followed swiftly by the League of Nations' condemnation of Italy as an aggressor and the imposition of economic sanctions.

It was agreed that a ban on exports to Italy would be imposed but certain key goods were excluded, including vital resources such as oil, coal, iron

and steel. Mussolini later claimed that had oil been included, he 'would have been obliged to withdraw from Abyssinia within a week', although this may be another instance of Mussolini's tendency to exaggerate.

The Hoare–Laval Pact

The status of the League was dealt a massive blow in December when details of a proposed Anglo–French deal with Italy were leaked to the press. The French Foreign Minister, Pierre Laval, and his British counterpart, Sir Samuel Hoare, had met in Paris and agreed a plan that they believed would appease Mussolini and restore peace. Italy would receive large areas of the most fertile, northerly part of Abyssinia, while the rest of the country would be a zone for future Italian economic expansion. In exchange, Abyssinia would receive part of Eritrea to provide the landlocked country with access to the sea. When the story broke, *The Times* derided this strip of land as 'a corridor for camels' and the name stuck.

The Hoare–Laval Pact caused an outcry in both countries as soon as the details emerged. The Foreign Ministers of the two main League powers had resorted to secret negotiations, in defiance of their League obligations, and in a manner which undermined what the League was trying to do.

Source 6.1

The three figures on the right of the picture represent (from left to right): France, Britain and Italy

Source 6.2

As Low recognised in March 1938, rearmament was one of the consequences of the failure of collective security during the Abyssinia crisis.

AH, IT WOULD HAVE BEEN CHEAPER HAD SHE LIVED.   (Copyright in All Countries.)

They were also planning to sacrifice the independence and security of a member state in order to appease Italy, a country which had defied the League's commitment to the peaceful resolution of disputes.

When details of the Pact emerged, the British cabinet refused to back Hoare's appeasement plan and he was forced to resign. Anthony Eden replaced him as Foreign Secretary. In France, Laval also had to resign.

Meanwhile, the war in Abyssinia continued. The Italians demonstrated the horrors of modern warfare by using poison gas and bombing raids against defenceless native settlements. On 5 May, the Italians entered the capital, Addis Ababa, and Emperor Haile Selassie was forced to flee. Two months later, the League lifted the sanctions imposed on Italy.

International consequences

The consequences of the Abyssinian War were far reaching:

1. Collective Security had been tested again – and failed. The reputation of the League was in tatters. After 1936 neither the British nor the French governments placed any faith in the League's ability to keep the peace, although there were still keen supporters of the League in both countries.

2. The Stresa Front had been destroyed. Italy no longer looked to France and Britain as natural allies. Instead, the two fascist powers drew closer together. By the autumn of 1936, the Rome–Berlin Axis would provide a formal recognition of that friendship.

3. Hitler was encouraged by the obvious reluctance of the British and French to take action to prevent aggression.

4. Differences between Britain and France were emphasised: the British government felt that Laval had encouraged Mussolini.

By 1936, the concept of collective security was to all intents and purposes dead because the League had not proved up the task when faced with naked aggression.

Source question practice

Source A

Sir Samuel Hoare had recently become Foreign Secretary and he (made) a bold speech in which he gave uncompromising adherence to all of the principles of the League. Those who still had faith in it had been encouraged. If we had then followed up these words with action, if we had unhesitatingly imposed every economic sanction ourselves, by a blockade prevented others from assisting Italy, closed the Suez canal to Italian shipping and at the same time mobilised the fleet, we should have rendered it quite impossible for Italy to continue the war unless she had been prepared to use force against Great Britain.

From Duff Cooper, *Old Men Forget*. The author was Secretary of State for War in 1935.

1 How far do you accept **Source A's** view of the British response to the Italian invasion of Abyssinia?

Use the Source and recalled knowledge.

The reoccupation of the Rhineland, 1936

Introduction

In March 1936, Hitler deliberately violated the terms of the Treaty of Versailles and moved German troops into the demilitarised Rhineland zone. This is known as 'the reoccupation of the Rhineland'. In Germany, there was overwhelming support for this move. Although both Britain and France protested, and the League of Nations condemned Germany's actions, nothing was done to stop Hitler. In Britain, in particular, there was a widespread belief that it was best to 'appease' Germany, in order to avoid the possibility of war. Nevertheless, there were already some outspoken critics of appeasement.

The status of the Rhineland

The Treaty of Versailles (1919)

One of the main aims of the Treaty of Versailles was to ensure that Germany would never again be in a position to launch a sudden attack on Belgium and France.

Articles 42 and 43 forbade Germany to station any troops, or to construct any military fortifications, in the Rhineland. In addition, Allied troops were to occupy the area on the left bank of the Rhine for fifteen years.

Source 7.1

ARTICLE 42
Germany is forbidden to maintain or construct any fortifications on the left bank of the Rhine or on the right bank to the west of a line drawn 50 kilometres to the East of the Rhine.

ARTICLE 43
In the area defined above the maintenance and the assembly of German armed forces, either permanently or temporarily, and military manoeuvres of any kind, as well as the upkeep of all permanent works for mobilisation, are in the same way forbidden.

From the Treaty of Versailles, 1919

Even these terms did not really satisfy the French. Clemenceau, the French Prime Minister in 1919, would have preferred an independent Rhineland Republic which would have provided France with greater security from attack.

The Locarno Treaties and the Rhineland Pact (1925)

By the mid-1920s relations between Germany, Britain and France were somewhat less strained. In October 1925, representatives of seven European countries met at Locarno, in southern Switzerland, and for the first time since the end of the war, Britain (represented by Sir Austen Chamberlain), France (represented by Aristide Briand) and Germany (represented by Gustav Stresemann) met on relatively friendly terms (see Chapter 2). As part of the Locarno Treaties the key participants agreed to sign a Treaty of Mutual Guarantee, more commonly known as the Rhineland Pact.

This Rhineland Pact confirmed Germany's frontiers with Belgium and France as established at Versailles, including the demilitarisation of the Rhineland. It stated that Germany and Belgium, and Germany and France, would not attack each other or resort to war against each other, except in legitimate self-defence. The terms of the Pact stated clearly that 'legitimate

Source 7.2

Post-war Europe, 1919

self-defence' would include the deliberate violation of the demilitarisation of the Rhineland. It seemed that by signing the agreement Germany now accepted the terms imposed in 1919.

In the improved atmosphere of post-Locarno Europe, Allied troops were gradually withdrawn from the Rhineland. The last French troops left in 1930, five years earlier than had originally been intended.

The French remained anxious about the possibility of a German attack across the Rhine, however, and in 1929 the French government began the construction of the Maginot Line to strengthen their eastern defences. This was a series of vast, state of the art underground defensive fortifications, built at huge cost over a number of years.

German attitudes to the demilitarisation of the Rhineland

Many Germans bitterly resented the demilitarisation of the Rhineland. They saw it as a significant aspect of the national humiliation inflicted on Germany by the hated Treaty of Versailles, arguing that the demilitarised Rhineland left their country vulnerable to attack.

From its earliest days the Nazi Party had demanded the 'revocation of the peace treaties of 1919', including, of course, the demilitarisation of the Rhineland.

Once in power, it was not long before Hitler was talking privately about the remilitarisation of the Rhineland. By November 1935, the French Ambassador in Berlin reported back to Paris that Hitler had made up his mind that he would reoccupy the Rhineland and was only waiting for a suitable opportunity. Nor was it just the Nazi Party that believed that one day Germany would again be able to station troops in the Rhineland and erect military fortifications in what was, after all, its own territory. The historian Ian Kershaw believes that 'the remilitarisation of the Rhineland would have been on the agenda of any German nationalist government and not just that of the Nazi Party'.

The attitude of the other major European powers

At the end of December 1935, in the wake of the Hoare–Laval Pact fiasco, Anthony Eden had replaced Hoare as Foreign Secretary. Eden believed Germany posed a major threat to European security: one of the first memos he prepared for the cabinet was entitled 'The German Danger'. Eden argued that Britain must speed up its rearmament programme, while at the same time

The reoccupation of the Rhineland, 1936

seeking some kind of agreement with Hitler. It was recognised that an 'agreement' would have to include concessions to Nazi Germany. A cabinet committee was set up to investigate further the possibility of reaching a settlement. It soon became clear that Eden was prepared to offer the remilitarisation of the Rhineland as part of a deal with Hitler. As one observer put it, the demilitarised zone in the Rhineland was a 'lost cause'.

Although Eden was later to be a prominent opponent of appeasement, early in 1936 he was prepared to negotiate with Hitler, and concede to Germany the right to remilitarise the Rhineland as long as he believed it would lead to a 'final' settlement of Germany's demands.

If Eden appeared to have abandoned the idea of retaining the Rhineland as a demilitarised zone, the situation in France was more confused. French society was deeply divided (see Chapter 5) and the Franco–Soviet Pact had intensified those divisions, with left-wing parties supporting the Pact and right-wing parties opposing it. When Laval was forced to resign, a stop-gap government was formed. There would be elections in the near future and there were few people in France who were prepared to risk foreign involvement without the full support of other European powers.

As far as Italy was concerned the invasion of Abyssinia marked the end of the Stresa Front and friendship with Britain and France. Italy needed an ally in Europe. In January 1936 Mussolini made it clear that he would not oppose a closer relationship between Germany and Austria in the future, and a little while later he indicated that Italy would not object if Germany was to reoccupy the Rhineland.

Why did Hitler choose to reoccupy the Rhineland in March 1936?

Even if we accept that Hitler was determined to achieve the reoccupation of the Rhineland at some point, we still have to explain why he chose to take action in March 1936. After all, it seemed highly likely that remilitarisation could have been achieved through negotiation within a very few years, given the attitude of the British government, and the reluctance of the French to act without British support.

In early 1936, the situation abroad was certainly favourable. Given Hitler's anti-communist views, the fact that in February 1936 the French parliament was in the process of ratifying the Franco–Soviet Pact gave him an additional excuse. Ian Kershaw, however, argues that it was not just developments outside Germany that determined the timing of Hitler's move.

> *In early 1936 domestic as well as foreign policy considerations almost certainly played a big part in the timing of Hitler's next gamble: to destroy what was left of the Versailles and Locarno Treaties by reoccupying the demilitarised Rhineland.*
>
> Ian Kershaw, Hitler 1889–1936: Hubris, 1998

The fact was that the economic situation in Germany was creating huge problems for the Nazi government, which was committed to an expensive rearmament programme. Rearmament necessitated imported raw materials, which had to be paid for using Germany's limited foreign currency reserves. At the same time ordinary German people, especially in the cities, were complaining bitterly about rising food prices. Wages were low and many families were living below the poverty line.

By the winter of 1935, police reports from various cities made it clear that the mood of the people was worryingly hostile to the government. Hitler was fully aware of the situation. He was determined to push ahead with rearmament but knew that his government could not afford to lose the support of large numbers of ordinary people – the very people who had voted for the Nazis in the first place. Good news – such as a success in foreign policy – would be a welcome way of distracting attention from the grim situation at home.

Source 7.3

German troops crossing the Rhine at Cologne 7 March 1936

The reoccupation of the Rhineland, 1936

51

Ian Kershaw reaches this conclusion:

> *Hitler needed no convincing of the domestic advantages and propaganda capital to be made from a dramatic national triumph... The sagging morale could be dispelled overnight, Hitler's own popularity still further enhanced... As, on other occasions, domestic and foreign policy considerations were closely intertwined in Hitler's thinking. International circumstances, opened up an opportunity to strike which Hitler felt he could not miss.*
>
> Ian Kershaw, *Hitler 1889–1936: Hubris*, 1998

German troops reoccupy the Rhineland

On 7 March, the Reichstag deputies packed the Kroll Opera House, where they had been meeting since the Reichstag fire of 1933. Hitler's speech to the deputies was broadcast to the nation. Not surprisingly, Hitler condemned the Franco–Soviet Pact and the prospect of an alliance with communism. He claimed that the French had violated the Locarno agreements and, as a result, Germany was no longer bound by the terms of the Rhineland Pact. Then he broke the news: as he spoke, German troops were entering the Rhineland. He justified his decision with these words:

> *In the interests of the primitive rights of a people to the security of its borders and safeguarding of its defence capability, the German Reich government has from today restored the full and unrestricted sovereignty of the Reich in the demilitarised zone of the Rhineland.*

The American journalist, William Shirer, who was present, reported that at this point the deputies leapt to their feet, giving the Nazi salute and shouting 'Heil Hitler!'

> *They spring, yelling and crying, to their feet. The audience in the galleries does the same, all except a few diplomats and about fifty of us correspondents. Their hands are raised in slavish salute, their faces now contorted with hysteria, their mouths wide open, shouting, shouting, their eyes, burning with fanaticism, glued on the new god, the Messiah. The Messiah plays his role superbly.*

At the same time, Hitler made an offer of peace, although he must have known that it was unlikely to be accepted. As the historian Arthur Marwick put it, 'The carrot as well as the stick was flourished'. Hitler proposed:

- a twenty-five year non-aggression pact with France and Belgium
- the return of Germany to the League of Nations
- a new demilitarised zone, which would extend both sides of the border between France and Germany. This would mean that the French would have to dismantle the Maginot Line, which Hitler knew would be completely unacceptable to the French.

Later Hitler apparently claimed, 'The forty eight hours after the Rhineland were the most nerve-wracking in my life. If the French had then marched into the Rhineland we would have had to withdraw with our tail between our legs, for the military resources at our disposal would have been wholly inadequate for even a moderate resistance'. The fact was, however, that the German troops who entered the Rhineland met with no resistance.

The international reaction to the reoccupation of the Rhineland

By the beginning of 1936, it was recognised in both Paris and London that Hitler was determined to achieve the remilitarisation of the Rhineland in the near future. The British government hoped that the issue could be settled as part of a negotiated settlement with Germany; the French government wanted to ensure that, if Hitler did order troops into the Rhineland, then Britain, Belgium and France – the Locarno Powers – would act together to stop the Germans. Nevertheless, the actual timing of the remilitarisation took both governments by surprise.

The French response

When German troops reoccupied the Rhineland, French society was deeply divided, so there was no shared response to the crisis. Right-wing parties, and their supporters, feared the spread of communism and were deeply opposed to the Franco–Soviet Pact, which they believed had provoked German anger unnecessarily. The parties of the left had recently overcome some of their differences and formed the Popular Front, which included the French Communist Party, a move that had served to increase the fears of the right. Elections in the near future meant that the neither right nor left would want to take the risk of plunging France into war.

The French army had grossly overestimated both the scale of German rearmament and the number of German soldiers involved in the reoccupation. General Gamelin, the Chief of Staff, told French ministers that a general mobilisation of the whole French army would be needed and that this was likely to lead to a long, drawn-out war. Gamelin urged that France should not act without the support of Britain and Belgium, who had also signed the Rhineland Pact. This treaty had justified action in the

case of 'flagrant aggression', but was remilitarisation really 'flagrant aggression'? Gamelin suggested that if France acted alone, then the League of Nations might condemn it as an aggressor.

Many historians argue that the building of the Maginot Line had affected French military thinking. With the massive line of fortifications in place, the army thought more in terms of defence than attack; therefore the generals were unable to plan a speedy reaction to German troop movements just over the border in Germany.

As a result, the French took no immediate action. Instead they called for a meeting of the Council of the League of Nations. In the meantime, the British Foreign Secretary, Anthony Eden, went to Paris to discuss the matter with the French government. Over the next few days, the French were won round to the British government's point of view.

The British response

The British government's reaction to the remilitarization of the Rhineland was largely determined by decisions made before 7 March. In January 1936, the Cabinet Defence Requirements Committee met to discuss future defence spending. Their deliberations made it clear that, despite some rearmament since the collapse of the disarmament conference, Britain was not ready for war. As the biographers of the Prime Minister, Stanley Baldwin, put it, 'Consciousness of Britain's unreadiness for war... affected both Baldwin and the Foreign Office in the months that followed and... fettered Eden's diplomacy' (Middlemas and Barnes, *Baldwin: A Biography*, 1969).

The Cabinet recognised that Britain's armed forces could not cope with all the demands that might be made of them and there was talk of 'limited liability'. The crisis surrounding the Italian invasion of Abyssinia seemed the most urgent problem facing the country and there were already concerns that the British armed forces were overstretched in the Mediterranean as a result of Italy's actions. When the Chiefs of Imperial General Staff – the heads of the Army, Navy and Air force – were consulted on 12 March, they made it clear that the armed forces were not in a position to fight a successful war against Germany.

Given that Britain was not ready for war, the Foreign Secretary, Anthony Eden, argued that Britain should try to negotiate some kind of 'final settlement' with Germany. By the middle of February 1936, Eden was already contemplating the possibility of including a negotiated remilitarization of the Rhineland in any such settlement with Germany. He wrote:

> *It seems undesirable to adopt an attitude where we would either have to fight for the (demilitarized) zone or abandon it in the face of a German reoccupation. It would be preferable for Great Britain and France to enter betimes into negotiations… for the surrender on conditions of our rights in the zone, while such a surrender still has got a bargaining value.*
>
> Anthony Eden, Facing the Dictators, 1962

In early March, Eden was at the League of Nations' headquarters in Geneva to discuss oil sanctions against Italy. There he met the French Foreign Minister, M Flandin, who made clear his concerns about the future of the Rhineland. When Eden reported Flandin's concerns to the British Cabinet on 5 March, Baldwin stated that 'the reality was that neither France nor England was really in a position to take effective military action against Germany in the event of a violation of the treaty of Locarno'.

The government's acceptance of the need to negotiate with Hitler reflected a widespread belief in Britain that the Rhineland was German territory, and that the terms of the Treaty of Versailles had been unduly harsh in this respect. After 7 March, many people were of the opinion that it was time to move on. A taxi driver, taking Eden to a meeting at No 10 Downing

Source 7.4

This Low cartoon from July 1936 shows that Low recognised the dangers of appeasing Hitler. From the right, the first two spineless leaders are Anthony Eden and Stanley Baldwin.

STEPPING STONES TO GLORY.

The reoccupation of the Rhineland, 1936

Street, voiced a widely held view when he remarked: 'I suppose that Jerry can do what he likes in his own back garden, can't he?' On 9 March, *The Times*' editorial comment, headed 'A Time to Rebuild', took a sympathetic view of the reoccupation. The editor of this influential 'establishment' newspaper argued that the Franco–Soviet Pact threatened German interests and that there was an important difference between the occupation of parts of one's own country and an attack on a neighbouring country.

Such views reflected most people's overwhelming desire for peace. In Parliament, the Labour Party remained committed to the peaceful resolution of disputes and to disarmament. During the debates on the reoccupation of the Rhineland in the House of Commons, a leading Labour MP, Hugh Dalton, declared, 'Public opinion in this country would not support, and certainly the Labour Party would not support, the taking of military sanctions, or even economic sanctions against Germany'. After all, Dalton went on to argue, Hitler's actions had taken place within Germany's own territory. It could not be classed as aggression in the way that Mussolini's invasion of Abyssinia undoubtedly was.

It would, however, be wrong to assume that in 1936 everyone favoured appeasement. In the House of Commons, Winston Churchill and Harold Macmillan pointed out the dangers of appeasing Hitler. In an article written for the *Star* newspaper, Macmillan did not hesitate to point out the possible long-term consequences of the failure to stop Hitler in 1936. He wrote:

> **"**
>
> *That is the tragic feature of the present crisis. There will be no war now. But unless a settlement is made now – a settlement which can only be made by a vigorous lead from this country – there will be war in 1940 or 1941.*

The League of Nations

On 14 March, the League of Nations Council met and declared that Germany had violated both the Treaty of Versailles and its Locarno commitments. The USSR suggested that sanctions should be imposed against Germany, which was in itself 'enough to damn the proposal' according to the historian AJP Taylor. A few days later, Britain, France and Belgium reaffirmed their Locarno Treaty commitments and invited Hitler to submit Germany's concerns about the Franco–Soviet Pact to the International Court at the Hague. Although this declaration seemed to satisfy people at the time, it amounted to very little. When Hitler rejected further proposals, it was clear that neither the League, nor the Locarno Powers, had achieved anything useful.

The significance of the Rhineland reoccupation for the future

Many historians have seen the reoccupation of the Rhineland as a turning point. The Treaty of Versailles and the Locarno settlement had been overthrown. As Ian Kershaw puts it, 'Locarno had been destroyed; Versailles was in tatters'.

Hitler had taken a considerable risk in March 1936. If the French had opposed the reoccupation with force, German troops would have had to withdraw. In fact, he had got away with it and this almost certainly encouraged him to look for further opportunities to extend Germany's power in Europe.

It was clear to Hitler that Britain was not prepared to enforce the terms of the Treaty of Versailles. In 1936, there was considerable support for the policy of appeasing Hitler: relatively few people saw how dangerous this was for the future. Again, this encouraged Hitler to believe that he could challenge other aspects of the peace treaties in the future.

The remilitarisation of the Rhineland made it much more difficult for the French to reach their allies in the east, which further undermined the French system of alliances. Germany was now in a much better position to attack eastwards without the risk of French intervention. As the historian William Carr put it, Hitler had 'closed the open flank in the west so that when the time came for Germany to move eastwards she would have no need to fear French reprisals'. In 1938 the Germans would start to build the Westwall, or Siegfried Line, to make their western border even more impenetrable.

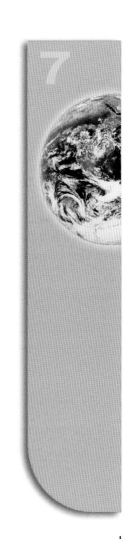

Activity

1. Create a spider diagram showing why the French government took no military action to stop Hitler's reoccupation of the Rhineland.

2. Create a second spider diagram showing the reasons for the British response. Are there any similarities?

3. What are the key differences between British and French reasons for not using military force to stop Hitler?

4. How do you explain the differences?

Source question practice

Source A

Looking back, it is easy to see clearly what many people knew then, that the successful remilitarisation of the Rhineland, in destroying the framework and the hopes of the interwar period, opened the way to all Hitler's outrages. Treaty links between East and West lost their meaning. Germany would have to be broken before the West could implement a guarantee to Poland, and by then it would be too late for other reasons. From 7 March, Hitler could carry out the programme he had defined in Mein Kampf ten years earlier... From 1936 onwards nearly all the smaller powers lost faith in the League of Nations.

From Elizabeth Wiskemann, *Europe of the Dictators*, 1966

Source B

The German reoccupation of the Rhineland marked the end of the devices for security which had been set up after the First World War. The League of Nations was a shadow; Germany could rearm, free from all treaty restrictions; the guarantees of Locarno were no more. Wilsonian idealism and French realism had failed. Europe returned to the system, or lack of system, which had existed before 1914. Every sovereign state, great and small, again had to rely on armed strength, diplomacy and alliances for security.

From AJP Taylor, *The Origins of the Second World War*, 1961

Source C

From a letter written by Nigel Law, formerly a senior civil servant at the Foreign Office. 'Moley' was Mr Orme Sargent, a known opponent of appeasement.

9 March 1936

My dear Moley

The sentiment of the City is overwhelmingly pro-German. No doubt you expected as much. I confess I had never realised the depth of anti-French feeling which forms the background to all foreign policy judgements here. Naturally there are many degrees of this sentiment. The most extreme are the Daily Mail readers who repeat the parrot cry 'You can't keep down for ever a nation of 67 million'. Next come those who disregard the denunciation of Locarno and affirm the right of Germany to reoccupy the demilitarised zone. They look hopefully towards a new era in Europe based on the acceptance of Hitler's offer. It does not follow that these are the reactions of the country at large. I have seen too often the extent the views of the City differ from those of the country on foreign affairs to suppose that on this occasion they are identical.

The city always minimises dangers at first because financial risk is the father of political thought. Consequently it concentrates its attention on Hitler's new promises and chooses to forget breaches of past ones.

Yours ever,
Nigel.

1   Compare the views about the consequences of the reoccupation of the Rhineland given in **Sources A** and **B**.

Compare the content overall and in detail.

2   How useful is **Source C** as evidence of British attitudes towards appeasement at the time of the reoccupation of the Rhineland?

In reaching a conclusion you should refer to:

○   *the origin and possible purpose of the source*

○   *the content of the source*

○   *recalled knowledge.*

The reoccupation of the Rhineland, 1936

The Spanish Civil War

Introduction

At first sight, the Spanish Civil War has little to do with the other European powers. Spain was no longer one of the big powers, and the roots of the terrible conflict which engulfed the country for nearly three years lay deep in Spain's past. However, the civil war quickly became the major battleground between fascism and communism. It was also seen by many outside Spain as a struggle between democracy and dictatorship. Both Hitler and Mussolini intervened in Spain for a variety of reasons, and the British and French reactions to this were motivated mainly by self interest and a desire to avoid the spread of the conflict.

Background information

By 1900, Spain was in serious decline. Most of its empire, which had once included most of South and Central America, had gone. A disastrous war with the USA in 1898 resulted in the loss of its remaining wealthy colonies in Cuba and the Philippines, and a long-running struggle against rebels in Spanish Morocco was a huge drain on the Spanish taxpayer.

Spain remained a largely rural society, dominated by wealthy landowners and the conservative Catholic church. Spanish politics was corrupt and there were massive inequalities between rich and poor.

The majority of Spaniards were very poor, especially the landless farm workers who worked on the big estates or *latifundia*. These *braceros* numbered perhaps 2.5 million and had no job security, were frequently starving and completely dependent on the estate owners for casual employment. The growing working-class in cities such as Madrid, Barcelona and Valencia also suffered dire poverty.

Discontent increased in Spain throughout the 1920s, and in 1931 elections resulted in a huge support for a republic. King Alfonso XIII abdicated and went into exile.

Hopes that a new political system in Spain would result in improvements soon evaporated. Economic, social and political problems increased. Regional divisions within Spain, with some areas demanding separation, soon worsened. Spain descended into a downward spiral of violence and hatred which was to culminate in the military rebellion of July 1936 and the subsequent civil war.

In the words of a modern historian of Spain, 'The coming of the Republic signified a threat to the most privileged members of society and raised inordinate hope amongst the humble' (Paul Preston, *A Concise History of the Spanish Civil War*, 1996).

The first Republican government did little but anger the traditional ruling powers, namely the Catholic Church, the rich *latifundia* owners and the officer class of the army. By 1934, the political pendulum swung and a more right-wing, conservative government came to power. Their policies reversed some of the previous government's reforms. Now the left-wing supporters of change were angry.

Tensions increased as political developments in the rest of Europe were mirrored in the polarisation of Spanish politics. On the right, the Falange Espanol was founded by Jose Antonio de Rivera. It copied many of the ideas and tactics of Hitler and Mussolini.

On the political left, anarchism gained supporters. The Anarchist movement despised all authority, not just the church, the army and the landowners but also parliaments and elections. They wanted to destroy all central authority and set up a society based on self-governing local communes.

Spanish politics were becoming increasingly extreme and yet another election in February 1936 resulted in a new left-wing government. The Spanish right were incensed by the Popular Front victory (a coalition of all left-wing groups in Spain) and reacted with a campaign of violence and terrorism. Despite the fact that the new Popular Front government contained no communists, the right convinced themselves that Spain was on the verge of a Soviet-style revolution as had happened in Russia in 1917.

The outbreak of war

The Spanish Civil War, which began in July 1936, was fought between the Republicans, supporters of the legitimate elected government, and the Nationalists, who were supporters of the rebels. It dragged on for three years.

The election results in 1936 had provided the trigger for the Spanish Civil War and the resulting European intervention. In July, a military rebellion started, led by General Francisco Franco, who was in command of the Spanish Army of Africa, based in Morocco. There was a tradition in Spain of the army officers intervening in politics, and the conspirators hoped that their coup d'etat (takeover) would be quickly successful throughout the

The Spanish Civil War

country. Using aircraft supplied by Germany and Italy, Franco organised an airlift of elite Spanish troops across the straits of Gibraltar to mainland Spain in early August, which probably saved the military rebellion from failure. At the end of the first week of August, 15,000 troops had been airlifted or ferried to mainland Spain, thanks to the dictators. This was the first decisive foreign intervention in the Spanish Civil War. Franco's Army of Africa was by far the most effective and feared fighting force involved in the struggle.

However, Franco and his supporters did not achieve the quick victory they hoped for.

Why did countries outside Spain get involved in the Spanish Civil War?

Some foreign countries saw the situation in Spain as part of the international struggle between democracy and fascism, or communism and capitalism. Others saw the civil war as a situation they could gain advantages from. Either way, the actions, or inaction, of foreign powers helped prolong the civil war.

Germany, Italy and Portugal all supported Franco's Nationalists, mostly for reasons of self interest. Spain and the issues within the Spanish Civil War became less important when compared to the advantages foreign powers might gain from the war.

Hitler believed a Nationalist victory would give him another potential ally against France and Britain. He also wanted access to Spanish raw materials, especially iron ore, to boost rearmament. More immediately Hitler realised he could use Spain as a training and testing ground for his growing army and air force.

Source 8.1

Major General von Richthofen, of the German Condor Legion, and General Franco

Mussolini also saw the Spanish Civil War as helpful to his ambitions. He hoped that a victory for Franco would gain Italy important naval bases in the Balearic islands (Majorca, Minorca and Ibiza), and so help in Italy's aim to dominate the Mediterranean. Mussolini also saw the Nationalist side as representing a similar movement to Italian Fascism, so he could not allow Franco to lose. More generally, Mussolini believed intervention in Spain would impress Hitler and show that Italy was an indispensable ally.

Both Hitler and Mussolini were quite happy to let the war drag on as a distraction for Britain and France and as a means of weakening opposition to the aggressive policies of Germany and Italy elsewhere. Tactically, Hitler was well aware of the advantages of having three fascist powers bordering France to the north, the east and the south. Hitler believed France could be trapped in a 'fascist triangle'.

Portugal had a right-wing military government under General Salazar, which shared many of the ideas and policies of the Nationalists. Salazar did not want a democratic or communist Spain on Portugal's doorstep.

What aid did the Nationalists get and was it decisive?

The German and Italian airlift of Franco's Army of Africa in August 1936 has already been mentioned. There were several other instances of when help given to the Nationalists was decisive.

Italy provided large amounts of arms and soldiers. As many as 75,000 Italian troops fought in Spain, with a maximum strength of 47,000. 5,000 were killed. Mussolini also sent aircraft and used his submarines to sink Republican shipping.

Germany sent the Condor Legion, comprising nearly 100 aircraft, including bombers. A total of 14,000 men served in the Condor Legion, with 300 being killed. The Germans provided the Nationalists with expert advice on modern weaponry, as well as supplying 200 tanks and 600 aircraft over the course of the conflict.

Portugal sent about 20,000 'volunteers', who were mostly regular soldiers. More importantly, the Portuguese government allowed the import of arms and other supplies through the common land border with Spain, which was mostly Nationalist-controlled.

By November 1936, help from both Germany and Italy allowed the Nationalists almost to capture Madrid. The Condor Legion provided the Nationalists with massive air superiority in northern Spain in the spring and summer of 1937. This enabled them, following the destruction of the historic Basque town of Guernica by bombers of the Condor Legion, to conquer the northern Basque provinces and the rest of the region by the autumn.

In March and April 1938, a Nationalist offensive, supported by 1,000 German and Italian aircraft and 200 tanks, cut the Republicans in two, separating Catalonia from the rest of their territory. Therefore, at decisive points in the war, help from Germany and Italy tipped the balance in favour of Franco and the Nationalists.

Republican aid

The Republicans received help from the Soviet Union and Mexico. Foreign volunteers also came to fight for the Republicans in large numbers. Most were organised into the Communist-led 'International Brigades'.

Soviet Russia

It seems odd to claim that Stalin, the Soviet communist dictator, did not want a communist Spain but it is true. Stalin's main foreign policy aim for most of this period was to co-operate with France and Britain against Nazi Germany. A communist victory in Spain would only serve to anger Britain and make Russian–British cooperation impossible to achieve. However, Stalin was also anxious for the Republic to avoid defeat and so keep the

Source 8.2

Men came from all over the world to fight for the Republican side

Axis powers bogged down in Spain for as long as possible. He drove a very hard bargain with the Republicans in return for aid. Soviet arms supplies were paid for in gold by the Bank of Spain. 500 Soviet advisers helped to recruit and train the Popular Army, which gradually replaced the hastily formed Republican militias, but no troops were sent. Heavy tanks and fighter aircraft started to arrive in late 1936, and undoubtedly helped the Republic to stave off defeat, but at no time during the war was Soviet aid enough to achieve victory.

Mexico

Mexico was too poor to provide any meaningful financial or military support, but identified with the Republican cause as the Mexicans had recently had a revolution of their own which had achieved some land reform and undermined the privileged position of the Catholic Church.

The International Brigades

Many foreigners identified strongly with the Republican side. Most of these volunteers were ordinary workers who welcomed a chance to fight against what they saw as Fascism. There were also intellectuals who gave massive publicity to the Republican cause. Most volunteers were organised in Paris by the Comintern. The Comintern was short for Communist International, a Soviet Russian controlled organisation for spreading communism worldwide.

It is estimated that a total of 40,000 volunteers fought for the Republic, although the maximum strength of the brigades in Spain was at most 20,000. The bulk were French, or German and Italian refugees who had left their homelands to escape political persecution, and welcomed an opportunity to fight back. About 2,300 British men served in the brigades, including 500 from Scotland. In total, 540 British 'brigaders' were killed.

The brigades helped in the defence of Madrid in November 1936, but their effect for the Republicans was perhaps more symbolic — it was a huge propaganda boost to morale. Only after serious Soviet aid ended were the brigades disbanded and sent home in autumn 1938.

A British artist, Jason Gurney, explained the motivation of many:

> The Spanish Civil War seemed to provide the chance for a single individual to take a positive and effective stand on an issue which appeared to be absolutely clear. Either you were opposed to the growth of Fascism and went out to fight against it, or you acquiesced in its crimes and were guilty of permitting its growth.
>
> Quoted in Paul Preston, A Concise History of the Spanish Civil War, 1996

The attitude of Britain and France

Public opinion in both countries was divided over the Spanish Civil War. In Britain, many intellectuals and trade unionists sympathised with the Republic (see above), but much of the business community and the Conservative Party were inclined to support the Nationalists. Reports of violence against priests and nuns by Republican supporters turned many religious people, especially Catholics, against the Republic. Most British people simply wished to avoid involvement in a brutal conflict which could easily spread outside Spain's borders.

In France, a Popular Front government similar to that in Spain, was elected in June 1936. Leon Blum, the new Prime Minister, was inclined to support the Republic, but was aware of how divisive this could be. He decided that help could only be given with British backing, which was unlikely. Therefore, he hit on the idea of non-intervention. If all the important European powers agreed not to intervene, Blum reasoned, the Republic would be victorious.

The British government agreed with the French view, but had other less noble motives. There were many British business interests in Spain, and these investors believed that their money was at risk if the Republicans won. Franco's tough anti-trade union stance was much more to their liking. The British business community had close links with the Conservative Party, which dominated the government. Many British supporters of the Republic believed that there was a conspiracy behind the government policy of non-intervention. Franco was easily able to get credit from the National Westminster Bank to buy weapons, while the Republic – the legally constituted government of Spain – was unable to obtain any loans from the Bank of England.

A British International Brigade veteran, recalling British government policy in 1986, stated:

> The so-called Non-Intervention policy was intervention in favour of Franco. The Republic of Spain was (an elected) Government recognised internationally as being the legitimate Government of the Spanish people. To prevent them from getting arms, purchasing arms, which they were prepared to do and pay for them, was of course simply part of the sabotage of the opposition to Franco and bolstering up the Franco regime... Franco would never have existed for any length of time, if the so-called Non-Intervention policy, supported by the British and the French, hadn't occurred.

Tom Murray, Voices from the Spanish Civil War, 1986

Neville Chamberlain became British Prime Minister in May 1937. He justified the Non-Intervention policy to the House of Commons:

> *Our policy has been consistently directed to one aim – to maintain the peace of Europe by confining the war to Spain. Although it is true that intervention has been going on and is going on, in spite of the non-intervention agreement, yet it is also true that we have succeeded in achieving the object at the back of our policy, and we shall continue that object and policy as long as we feel there is reasonable hope of avoiding the spread of the conflict...*
>
> *Although it may be true that various countries or various governments desire to see one side or the other side in Spain winning, there is not a country or a government that wants to see a European war.*
>
> *Neville Chamberlain, speech in the House of Commons, 22 February, 1938*

Historian AJP Taylor gives his view on British attitudes to the conflict:

> *Most people displayed little concern. They wanted peace. They disliked communism. Baldwin (and Chamberlain after him) gave them what they wanted.*
>
> *AJP Taylor, English History 1914–1945, 1965*

Non-Intervention

As a result of Blum's appeal on 1 August 1936, a total of sixteen countries had signed the Non-Intervention Pact by the end of the month, including Germany, Italy and Soviet Russia, agreeing to remain neutral in the conflict and not supply war materials. Blum's decision to close the border between France and Spain on 8 August was a serious blow to the Republic.

The first meeting of the Non-Intervention Committee took place in London on 9 September, 1936. However, it was quickly clear that Germany, Italy and Portugal were continuing to help the Nationalists. As a result, Soviet Russia announced its withdrawal from the agreement at the end of October, and began openly to send aid to the Republicans. It seemed as though the British and French policy was in ruins, but both governments continued with their efforts. On Christmas Eve 1936, they appealed to Germany, Italy, Portugal and Soviet Russia to stop supplying the two sides fighting in Spain. This was followed on 2 January 1937 by the so-called 'Gentleman's Agreement' in Rome between Britain and Italy to maintain the status quo in the western Mediterranean. It was hoped that Mussolini would agree to withdraw his 'volunteers' from Spain. At this

time, Britain and France still hoped to avoid closer German–Italian co-operation by maintaining friendly relations with Mussolini, despite all that had happened in Abyssinia.

However, the Italians continued to send troops and supplies to Franco. In February, Italy followed Britain and France in prohibiting its citizens from leaving to fight in Spain – but of course, this did not apply to those who were already there. Many British and French volunteers still travelled to Spain as tourists, joining the Republican forces on arrival. The writer George Orwell joined in this way.

In April 1937, the Non-Intervention Committee agreed to an international naval patrol of the coasts around Spain. The aim was to stop supplies reaching both sides, but it was soon clear that the German and Italian warships were only stopping Republican supplies, while continuing to aid the Nationalists. In frustration, Republican aircraft bombed the German warship *Deutschland* on 29 May, leading to the retaliatory bombardment of the Republican port of Almeria two days later. In June, the German cruiser *Leipzig* was attacked by submarines. Germany and Italy immediately announced their withdrawal from the naval patrol and hence the Non-Intervention Committee, and again openly supplied Franco. This, coupled with submarine attacks (widely thought to be Italian) on Republican shipping throughout the summer of 1937, suggested that the British and French policy of non-intervention was in ruins.

Nevertheless, the British continued to press ahead with various proposals, but it was only when the government ordered the Royal Navy to counter-attack in the event of submarine attacks on British merchant shipping that any progress was made. In September, at a conference in Nyon, Switzerland, the remaining non-intervention powers agreed to British and French naval patrols on the main Mediterranean routes. At the end of the month, the Italians reached an agreement with the committee and asked to join the Nyon Patrol, and submarine attacks ceased.

By this time, any realistic hope the British might have had that Mussolini could be persuaded away from Hitler was dashed when Italy joined the Anti-Comintern Pact on 6 November 1937. The following month, Mussolini announced Italy's withdrawal from the League of Nations.

In the summer of 1938, a detailed scheme of non-intervention, based on the previous year's plan, was agreed, including provision for the withdrawal of all volunteers. By this time, the fate of the Republic was more or less sealed. Defeat was now a matter of time. The British and French governments were more concerned with events in Austria and Czechoslovakia and it became clear that they had no further interest in the Spanish conflict since the outcome was inevitable.

Barcelona fell on 26 January 1939, leading to the complete conquest of Catalonia. Hundreds of thousands of refugees fled across the border to France to escape the wrath of Franco's forces. On 27 February, Britain and France recognised Franco's government even before the war had ended with the fall of Madrid at the end of March. On 1 April 1939, the war was officially declared to be over.

The impact of foreign intervention

Most historians agree that foreign intervention in the Spanish Civil War was more effective on the Nationalist side. Historian Paul Preston believes that the military rebellion would not have succeeded without German and Italian intervention:

> "
> *Mussolini and Hitler thus turned a coup d'etat going wrong into a bloody and prolonged civil war. Thirty Junkers JU-52 transport aircraft joined the Italian bombers and so permitted Franco to launch the first significant military airlift in history.*
>
> Paul Preston, A Concise History of the Spanish Civil War, 1996

Source 8.3

This Republican propaganda poster protests against the bombing of towns by German and Italian planes

In November 1936, the arrival of the German Condor Legion gave the Nationalists crucial superiority in aircraft and tanks. Franco was able to use this control of the air at vital moments. The Germans also gained important experience in the possible use of air power, which was put to good use during the early successful campaigns of the Second World War.

Although Mussolini sent considerable numbers of ground forces to Spain, their presence was often not very effective. Many units were poorly trained and equipped. Such deficiencies were hidden from the Italian public, and it was thought that Franco viewed his Italian allies with some contempt, although he said nothing publicly. However, the large amounts of aircraft, tanks and motor vehicles sent to Franco as a result of a secret treaty signed in November 1936, and shipped to Spain because of Italian naval strength in the western Mediterranean, undoubtedly gave a further boost to the Nationalists.

In the autumn of 1938, Hitler sent the Nationalists more aid in the aftermath of Munich, which helped Franco's final drive to victory. In return, the Germans were given exclusive rights to mine Spanish iron ore, thus boosting the rearmament programme.

As far as the Republicans were concerned, aid from Soviet Russia was the only help that made any difference. The impact of the International Brigades was mostly symbolic (see above), and historian Raymond Carr points out that after December 1936 there were always more Germans and Italians in Spain than International Brigaders. Carr also assesses the impact of Soviet supplies on the Republicans – 'Without them, the Republic would have gone under by early 1937, but they staved off defeat rather than underwrote victory' (Raymond Carr, *Images of the Spanish Civil War*, 1986).

To quote Preston on the impact of foreign intervention – or non-intervention – on the outcome of the war, 'Hitler, Mussolini, Franco and Chamberlain were responsible for the Nationalist victory, not Stalin.'

Why did Franco and the Nationalists win the Spanish Civil War?

You will probably have already worked out some reasons. There are broadly four main points to remember.

1) **Nationalist unity.** Fairly early on in the war, Franco was the undisputed leader, or *caudillo*. All the various Nationalist groups and parties were merged into one single party, the *Movimiento*, and Franco also had complete control of the army as well. He was a ruthless and determined leader, fighting for a unified, Catholic, authoritarian Spain.

2) **Republican disunity.** As a coalition of several democratic parties, it was always going to be more difficult for the Republicans to achieve a united leadership. Different groups had different aims – the Basques and the Catalans wanted to keep and extend their autonomy, the Socialists were split between reformists and revolutionaries who wanted a workers' state, the Anarchists only reluctantly wanted any government at all, and the Communists were totally under Stalin's control. These tensions severely weakened the Republican war effort, and led to fighting in Barcelona in May 1937 between the Anarchist-dominated militias and the Socialists and their Communist allies, in which 500 people died. The new government, under the Socialist Negrin, was increasingly under Soviet influence, and suppressed the militias, replacing them with a conscript army with proper military ranks. These divisions were a serious flaw for the Republicans, hampering their ability to wage a successful war.

3) **Foreign Intervention.** This has been discussed in detail above. Most historians agree that without the intervention of foreign powers, the Republic would probably have won. The military coup had been defeated in most of the major centres of population, and it was only the airlift of the Army of Africa to the mainland from Morocco that transformed the failed coup into a civil war.

4) **Non-Intervention.** As the legally elected government of Spain, the Republic should have had the right to purchase arms on the international market. The British and French policy of non-intervention denied them this by treating both sides as equal. Given the more effective military aid given to Franco, it is clear that non-intervention worked against the Republicans and so was a major cause of their defeat.

The consequences of the Spanish Civil War for Spain

The effect on Spain was disastrous. Perhaps 600,000 people died during the war, either from military action or politically-motivated executions. Franco governed Spain as though it was an occupied country. It was estimated that 10,000 people were killed in Madrid alone in the five months following the end of the war. Perhaps two million Republican supporters were imprisoned between 1939 and 1942. Executions continued until the 1940s. The Spanish economy was devastated, taking many years to recover. Franco had little real option but to remain neutral when the Second World War broke out scarcely six months after the end of the struggle in Spain, despite his debt of gratitude to Hitler and Mussolini. Only after Franco's death in 1975, did Spain move towards democracy. For many on the political left in Spain, the Civil War has left a bitter legacy which has still not been fully confronted.

The consequences of the Spanish Civil War for Europe

Britain's policy of Non-Intervention was motivated by its anxiety to avoid the spread of war. The fact that its inevitable outcome was a Nationalist victory was not a major concern for the British government. Involvement in Spain led to increased co-operation between Germany and Italy. Mussolini was actually weakened by the poor performance of his forces, and was forced to depend on Germany for support, thus ending any hopes that Britain and France had of keeping the dictators apart. For many people, the failure of non-intervention further discredited the appeasement policies of Britain and France, although Neville Chamberlain only admitted failure in March 1939 (see Chapter 10).

Activity

Remember that although there are no essay questions in the Special Topic, you can select your extended essay from any area of the course. You could consider the following question in light of this, as well as to help revise this chapter.

1 How important was foreign intervention in the Spanish Civil War?

Source question practice

1 Look at the quotes from Tom Murray, Neville Chamberlain and AJP Taylor on pages 66–7. Using these, describe how much support you think there was in Britain for the government's policy of non-intervention in Spain?

Use the sources and recalled knowledge.

2 How useful is the quote from Chamberlain on page 67 in explaining the reasons for the policy of non-intervention?

In reaching a conclusion you should refer to:

○ *the origin and possible purpose of the source*

○ *the content of the source*

○ *recalled knowledge.*

9 *Anschluss*: the annexation of Austria

Introduction

In March 1938, two years after the reoccupation of the Rhineland, Hitler achieved another of the Nazi Party's main aims. In defiance of the Treaty of Versailles, German troops marched into Austria and Hitler proclaimed union, or *Anschluss*, between the two countries. From then on the new *GrossDeutschland*, or 'Greater Germany', dominated the centre of Europe and threatened the independence of Czechoslovakia. Beyond Czechoslovakia lay the lands of Eastern Europe which many Nazis believed would provide suitable *lebensraum* for Germany.

Source 9.1

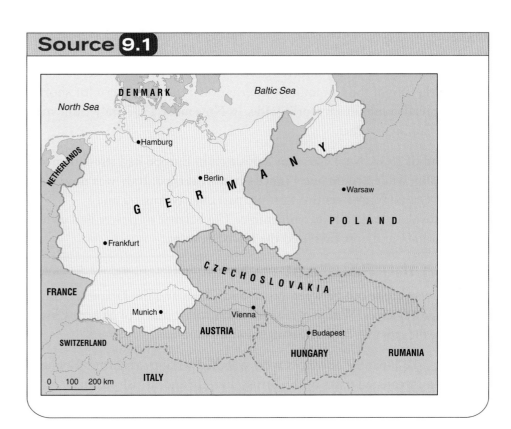

How did the international balance of power change between 1936 and 1938?

Important changes took place between 1936 and 1938. Not all of these were the direct result of German actions but they all worked in Hitler's favour in 1938.

The formation of the Rome–Berlin Axis and the Anti-Comintern Pact

By 1936, Mussolini's actions in Abyssinia had wrecked the short-lived Stresa Front and the two main fascist countries in Europe were drawing closer together. In October of that year the Italian Foreign Minister visited Berlin and the two countries signed an agreement known as the **Rome–Berlin Axis**. Although this was not a military alliance, it meant that Mussolini was less likely to oppose a German move to annex, or take over, Austria.

In November 1936 Germany signed an agreement with Japan. This was the **Anti-Comintern Pact,** an agreement to oppose the spread of communism and especially aimed against the USSR. Fascist powers believed the aim of the Communist International (or Comintern for short) was to spread communism world-wide. In November 1937 Italy came into the Anti-Comintern Pact.

By the end of 1937, Nazi Germany's position in Europe had strengthened considerably while Britain and France's had weakened. Italy was now a friend of Germany, and central Europe, particularly Austria and Czechoslovakia, looked to be vulnerable. The balance of power had swung against Britain and now favoured the fascist powers.

War in the Far East

In 1937, war broke out between Japan and China and the Japanese army made huge advances. Within a year they controlled much of eastern China, including the cities of Beijing, Shanghai and Nanjing.

In Britain, the Japanese advances were watched with great alarm. Japanese expansion threatened parts of the British Empire and British financial and commercial interests in the Far East. It was clear that the British armed forces were not strong enough to face up to an enemy in the east as well as possible enemies in Europe. This would have a major effect on British foreign policy.

A new Prime Minister in Britain

In May 1937, Stanley Baldwin announced his retirement, just a few months before his seventieth birthday. The new Prime Minister, Neville Chamberlain, would soon be closely associated with the policy of appeasement. Having lived through the horror of World War One, Chamberlain was determined to avoid war at almost any cost. In November 1937, he sent Lord Halifax to meet the leaders of Nazi Germany. Halifax returned home impressed by what he had seen. He wrote afterwards:

> *Although there was much in the Nazi system that profoundly offended British opinion, I was not blind to what Hitler had done for Germany, and to the achievement from his point of view of keeping Communism out of his country.*

Neville Chamberlain was the second son of Joseph Chamberlain, a successful Birmingham businessman who had been a reforming Mayor of Birmingham and then, later, a distinguished Cabinet Minister. It was not particularly surprising that Neville followed in his father's footsteps, first as a successful businessman, then as mayor of Birmingham and then, in later life, as an MP. His older half-brother, Austen, had already been an MP for many years when Neville entered the House of Commons as a Conservative in 1918.

Chamberlain held various government posts in the 1920s, and then in 1931 he was appointed Chancellor of the Exchequer in the National Government formed to tackle the problems of the Great Depression. He continued as Chancellor when Stanley Baldwin replaced Ramsey MacDonald as Prime Minister, and when Baldwin retired in May 1937, shortly before his seventieth birthday, Chamberlain succeeded him as Prime Minister. He was already 68 years old.

In February 1938, Anthony Eden resigned from his post as Foreign Secretary because he did not agree with Chamberlain's policy of appeasement. In his place Halifax became the new Foreign Secretary, so by early 1938 the two most important men in the British government were clearly committed to appeasing Hitler.

Developments within Germany

German rearmament continued to gather pace after the reoccupation of the Rhineland. The Four Year Plan drawn up by the Nazi government aimed to increase weapons production, as well as preparing the German economy for war.

The Four Year Plan increased pressure on the German economy. Supplies of raw materials were urgently needed and the historian Ian Kershaw argues that by the summer of 1937 'Hitler... was already beginning to turn his eyes towards Austria and Czechoslovakia' as a way of obtaining them. In July, Goebbels wrote in his diary: 'Austria is not a state at all. Its people belong to us and will come to us. The Fuhrer's entry into Vienna one day will be his proudest triumph.'

On 5 November 1937 Hitler called a meeting of the War Minister and the heads of the Armed Services. Colonel Hossbach, one of those present, jotted down some notes, and it is because the Americans found a version of these notes at the end of the war that we know what was discussed at this meeting.

According to Hossbach's notes, it was at this meeting that Hitler first talked to the Chiefs of Staff about the timing of German expansion into Austria and Czechoslovakia. Incorporating Austria and Czechoslovakia into the German Reich could provide food to feed millions more people, increase the size of the army and improve the security of Germany's frontiers. According to Hossbach's notes, Hitler declared that it was his 'unalterable determination to solve the German problem of space by 1943–45 at the latest'. He also stated that there were circumstances in which Germany should be ready to strike out against Austria and Czechoslovakia much earlier – even as early as 1938.

Historians do not agree about the significance of the Hossbach memorandum. Does it prove that from November 1937 onwards, Hitler was formulating plans for expansion into eastern Europe, with a clear timescale in mind? Or is this reading too much into a single meeting? The historian Ian Kershaw believes that, even if no precise plans had been drawn up, 'The Third Reich was entering a new, more radical phase. The drift of Hitler's thinking was plain' (Ian Kershaw, *Hitler 1936–1945: Nemesis*, 2001).

A few months later, the Austrian Chancellor, Kurt Schuschnigg, would provide Hitler with the perfect excuse to absorb Austria into the German Reich.

The background to *Anschluss*: Austro–German relations before 1934

Until 1918, German-speaking Austria was just one part of the vast, multi-ethnic Austro–Hungarian Empire. The Imperial family – the Habsburgs – ruled over a vast area of central and eastern Europe which reached right into the heart of the Balkans. Although German-speaking Vienna was the main Imperial city, few people had thought of union with other German-speaking people until the second half of the nineteenth century. However, as the various people of the Austro–Hungarian Empire demanded either independence or greater autonomy, many Austrian Germans began to argue that all Germans should be united in a single country. These Pan-Germans longed for a unified greater Germany – a *GrossDeutschland*.

The Austro–Hungarian Empire disintegrated as a result of World War One. As the victorious allies (Britain, France and the USA) negotiated separate treaties with the new countries which emerged from the wreck of the former Empire, many Austrians were deeply unhappy about the situation they found themselves in. Far from living in a powerful 'Greater Germany', they were citizens of a small and rather insignificant country with a population of 7 million, and a capital city – Vienna – out of all proportion to the size of the country. Moreover, union with Germany was forbidden for all time by the terms of the Treaty of Versailles.

It is hardly surprising, then, that many Austrians still longed for unification with Germany and watched the rise of the German Nazi Party with approval. By the early 1930s the Austrian wing of the Nazi Party was causing real problems for the government and in 1933 the Austrian Chancellor, Engelbert Dollfuss, banned both the Nazi Party and the Communists in an attempt to stabilise and retain control over the country.

July 1934: the assassination of Dollfuss

On 25 July 1934, Austrian Nazis managed to assassinate Dollfuss. They hoped that this would create such chaos that Hitler would intervene to restore order, and that *Anschluss* would follow.

Mussolini thought otherwise. Fearing that *Anschluss* would create a very powerful and potentially hostile neighbour immediately to the north of Italy, he moved troops into the border area making it clear that he would not tolerate German intervention. Since Germany did not yet have

sufficient armed forces to risk war, Hitler decided to do nothing. On this occasion Mussolini's intervention secured the survival of an independent Austria and a crisis was averted.

The agreement of July 1936

The new Austrian Chancellor, Kurt Schuschnigg, tried to cooperate as much as possible with Germany, to avoid giving Hitler the excuse to invade. In 1936 the two countries signed an agreement which Schuschnigg hoped would help preserve Austrian independence. Germany agreed to respect Austria's independence but Schuschnigg had to agree to bring Austrian foreign policy into line with Germany's. More significantly, the ban on the Nazi Party was lifted and Nazis were to be allowed to hold important positions in the Austrian government.

Anschluss

By the beginning of 1938 Hitler and his main ministers were determined to increase the pressure on Austria. By now they were confident that neither Britain nor Italy would do anything to defend Austria, and Göring, who was in charge of the Four Year Plan, was anxious to secure new sources of raw materials.

On 12 February Schuschnigg and Hitler met at the Berghof, Hitler's mountain retreat in the Alps near Berchtesgarten. Hitler launched into a furious verbal attack on the Austrian government. Using the methods of a bully, he threatened Schuschnigg:

And this I tell you, Herr Schuschnigg, I am firmly determined to make an end to all of this... I have an historic mission... Who knows? Perhaps I will appear sometime overnight in Vienna; like a spring storm. Then you'll see something.

Faced with the apparent threat of a German invasion of Austria, Schuschnigg agreed to:

- Lift all the remaining restrictions on the Austrian Nazi party.
- Release any Nazis who were held in prison.
- Appoint a leading Nazi, Arthur Seyss-Inquart, as Minister of the Interior, with control over the security forces.
- Appoint another Nazi, Glaisse-Horstenau, as Minister for War.

These demands almost completely undermined the independence of the Austrian government.

Having agreed to these terms, Schuschnigg returned home, where the Austrian Nazi Party continued to stir up trouble. As a result Schuschnigg had second thoughts about the recent agreement and on 9 March he announced a referendum, to be held four days later, in which Austrian voters would be asked to vote in favour of an independent Austria.

The German government was taken by surprise. Hitler, Göring and Goebbels discussed the situation late into the night. By the following morning, invasion plans were being drawn up. Eventually the German government decided to demand the cancellation of the plebiscite, the resignation of Schuschnigg and the appointment of Seyss-Inquart as Chancellor. At first the Austrian government refused to accept all of the terms but when Schuschnigg requested British help Lord Halifax replied that 'His Majesty's government are unable to guarantee protection'. By 3.30pm on the afternoon of 11 March Schuschnigg had resigned, realising he could expect no help from Britain or France. Even so, the Austrian President refused to appoint Seyss-Inquart as Chancellor.

Source 9.2

This cartoon by David Low appeared in the Evening Standard on 18 February 1938. Low is taking the minority anti-appeasement position. Many in Britain felt that Austria was far away and not Britain's problem. Look carefully at Low's cartoon and how he suggests that pressure on Austria would eventually cause problems for Britain.

INCREASING PRESSURE.

By late that afternoon Austrian Nazi supporters were rioting in the streets and occupying government buildings. In Berlin, frantic negotiations led to reassurances from Mussolini that Italy would accept German intervention in Austria. Finally at midnight, the Austrian President recognised that he had no other option and accepted the appointment of Seyss-Inquart as Chancellor.

All Hitler's demands had now been met, yet the invasion still went ahead. Early on 12 March 1938, German troops entered Austria, allegedly in response to a request from Seyss-Inquart. At 4pm Hitler himself crossed the German–Austrian border at Braunau am Inn, his birthplace, driven in an open-topped Mercedes, despite the freezing weather. Church bells rang to greet him and thousands of people flocked out into the streets to welcome the Fuehrer. Several hours later, Hitler reached Linz.

> "
> *Peals of bells rang out; the ecstatic crowd was screaming 'Heil'; Seyss-Inquart (who was there to greet Hitler) could hardly make himself heard in his introductory remarks. Hitler looked deeply moved. Tears ran down his cheeks. In his speech on the balcony of the Linz town hall, he told the masses, constantly interrupting him with their wild cheering, that Providence must have singled him out to return his homeland to the Reich… To the accompanying unending cries of 'One People, one Reich one Leader', Hitler decide to stay in Linz throughout the next day… and enter Vienna on the Monday.*
>
> Ian Kershaw, Hitler 1936–1945: Nemesis, 2001

It seems that Hitler's plans changed at this point. In Ian Kershaw's view, Hitler had not planned an immediate union between Austria and Germany but he was carried away by the moment and by the evident support for his government among the Austrian people. Until then, he had not intended to annex Austria immediately. The following day, however, a new law announced Austria's incorporation into the German Reich.

On 14 March Hitler arrived in Vienna. Vast crowds greeted him, church bells pealed and Nazi swastikas flew from the church steeples. The next day Hitler addressed a crowd of around 250,000 in the Heldenplatz in central Vienna. Although the Austrian Nazi Party made sure that there were large numbers of their supporters present, there was little doubt about the enthusiasm of many Austrians. That same evening, Hitler flew back to Germany, well pleased with the way in which things had turned out. Austria was now part of the Greater German Reich and none of the other European powers had done anything to prevent it.

Source 9.3

Austrians greeting Hitler's arrival in Vienna, March 1938

The consequences of *Anschluss* for Austria

On 10 April, the new government organised a plebiscite in which the people of Austria were asked whether they approved of *Anschluss*. The plebiscite was blatantly unfair: many voters were intimidated, Jews were not allowed to take part and numerous opponents of the regime had already been arrested. Even so, with over 99 per cent of voters in favour of *Anschluss*, the result seemed to show that most people supported the incorporation of Austria into the Greater German Reich.

The precise extent of Austrian support for the Nazi take-over is still a matter of debate. Some historians argue that the contemporary Nazi-controlled newsreels showing enthusiastic crowds and public celebrations do not tell the whole story about whether or not the majority of the people were happy about *Anschluss*.

Austria rapidly became a Nazi state. Within a few weeks, a concentration camp was established at Mathausen, so that more opponents of the new regime could be locked up. Discrimination against Jews, and other ethnic

Source 9.4

Austrian Jews faced humiliation and oppression. Here Jews in Vienna have been forced to scrub pavements

minorities, was widespread: in Vienna Jewish shops were boycotted and Jews were humiliated.

> *Groups of Jews, men and women, young and old, were dragged from offices, shops or homes and forced to scrub the pavements in 'cleaning squads', their tormentors standing over them, and watched by crowds of onlookers screaming 'Work for Jews at last', kicking them, drenching them with cold, dirty water, and subjecting them to every conceivable form of merciless humiliation.*
>
> Ian Kershaw, Hitler 1936–1945: Nemesis, 2001

Many Jews tried to flee to Prague, only to find that they were turned back at the frontier. Others committed suicide, believing that there was no other way of escaping Nazi brutality.

The consequences of *Anschluss* for Germany

The Austrian Army was incorporated into the German Army, which greatly increased the overall size of Germany's armed forces.

Germany could exploit Austrian resources and technical expertise.

Access to Eastern Europe, through Austria, was now much easier. The prospect of acquiring further *lebensraum* in the east was real.

'Greater Germany' now surrounded the western half of Czechoslovakia (the Sudentenland and Bohemia), making it easier for the German government to threaten Czechoslovakia in the future. If this should happen, then it would be almost impossible for Czechoslovakia's ally, France, to come to its aid.

For the first time, Hitler had used the German army outside Germany in order to achieve what he wanted.

Hitler's self confidence was increased. He had got away with *Anschluss* without being challenged by the West. Franz von Papen, then the German ambassador in Vienna, later claimed, 'The result was that Hitler became impervious to the advice of all those who wished him to exercise moderation in his foreign policy'.

The international response

France

The union of Austria and Germany went unchallenged by the international community. The French government had resigned a few days before and so, technically, France was without a government. Ministers threatened to call up reservists to strengthen France's army, but only if Britain approved. Since Britain did not respond, the French did nothing. By this time the Maginot Line was nearly complete, and the French were increasingly reliant on their ability to halt a German attack on France, should it occur.

Italy

When Schuschnigg had appealed to Italy for support on 11 March, on the eve of *Anschluss*, Mussolini had refused to answer the phone. The Italian government, which was increasingly dependent on German friendship, did not even protest when *Anschluss* took place.

The League of Nations

The League of Nations was so discredited after the failure of sanctions in Abyssinia that no member state referred the issue of Anschluss to the League of Nations.

How did Britain respond to *Anschluss*?

By early 1938, the British government was well aware that Hitler was planning closer ties with Austria. Nevertheless, the events of 11–13 March took ministers by surprise.

When Lord Halifax, the future Foreign Secretary, visited Berlin in November 1937, he had discussed the future of Austria with Hitler. He wrote afterwards that Hitler told him that 'Germany did not want to annex Austria…. Her desire was to bring about by peaceful means full, economic, cultural, commercial and possibly monetary and currency union with Austria and see in Austria a government really friendly to Germany'. Lord Halifax, for his part, assured Hitler that the Austrian question, like issues arising over Czechoslovakia and Danzig, 'fell into categories of possible alterations in the European order which might be destined to come about with the passage of time'. It was known that Halifax was close to Chamberlain and his visit convinced Hitler that Britain would not act to defend Austria.

Immediately after *Anschluss*, it became clear that Hitler was right. Britain would protest about what had happened – but it would do nothing more.

On 11 March, the British Ambassador in Berlin protested to the German Foreign Minister as soon as he heard that German troops were crossing the Austrian border. But as he himself later admitted, 'verbal protests without the resolute intention to use force were not going to stop the German troops'. Later in the day, he encountered Göring at the ballet in Berlin, and accused Germany of bullying Austria. But that was all that happened.

Three days later, Chamberlain made an official statement in the House of Commons. While he condemned Germany's actions and the way in which *Anschluss* had been imposed on Austria, he made it clear that 'the hard fact is… that nothing could have arrested this action by Germany unless we and others with us had been prepared to use force to prevent it'. At the same time, he acknowledged that the *Anschluss* had increased uncertainty in Europe and that the government would review its defence requirements in the light of recent events.

Chamberlain's response reflected the view of many ordinary people. According to Ian Kershaw:

> "
> *Neither the government nor British public opinion was ready to go to war over a country whose population comprised ethnic Germans, a good proportion of whom enthusiastically favoured union with Germany.*
>
> Ian Kershaw, Making Friends With Hitler, 2004

In the next few weeks, newspapers published many letters in support of *Anschluss*. Most emphasised the same points: the Austrians were ethnic Germans; Austria had been treated unfairly in 1919 and as a result, union with Germany seemed desirable; Schuschnigg had acted irresponsibly; the plebiscite held in April demonstrated how many Austrians approved of *Anschluss*. In an article written for the *Evening Times*, George Bernard Shaw, the well-known playwright, stated that:

> We may as well accept the Anschluss without grumbling, not only because it is an excellent thing in itself but because at Versailles we helped to create the situation which made it inevitable.
>
> — George Bernard Shaw

Not everyone was as complacent as Shaw, however. The anti-appeasers in the House of Commons were outspoken in their criticism of government policy. They pointed out that Hitler had deliberately violated the terms of the Treaty of Versailles. Austria was a separate, independent country which the Germans had invaded. They criticised the government for abandoning collective security. Above all, they argued that Hitler could not be trusted – having seized Austria, his next target would be Czechoslovakia.

Responding to Chamberlain's statement in the House of Commons, Clement Attlee, the Labour Party leader, demanded 'a return to League principles and League policy to build up a world of law and a world of justice'. The Liberal leader, Sir Archibald Sinclair, also argued that Britain should base its policies 'on the principles of the League of Nations'. But of all the anti-appeasers, Churchill was the most vehement. He too emphasised that Britain should enforce League principles. Failure to do so would result in other smaller countries being overwhelmed by Nazi Germany. He concluded by calling for a grand alliance of European countries opposed to Hitler's Germany.

> If a number of states were assembled around Great Britain and France in a solemn treaty for mutual defence against aggression; if they had their forces marshalled in what you might call a Grand Alliance... then I say that you might even now arrest this approaching war!
>
> Churchill in the House of Commons, 14 March 1938. Quoted in Alistair Parker, *Churchill and Appeasement*, 2000

Anschluss: the annexation of Austria

It is clear that Churchill and the other anti-appeasers had considerable support outside Parliament. An opinion poll revealed that of those questioned, more than half did not agree with Chamberlain's foreign policy (see Source 9.5).

Source 9.5

Gallup poll responses to the question: Do you support Chamberlain's foreign policy?

No opinion

Yes

No

Source 9.6

Low has shown Mussolini, Chamberlain, Lord Halifax and the French Prime Minister, Edouard Daladier, all prepared to accept what has happened to Austria, for fear of what might happen if they opposed it. The figure by the ballot box is Hitler's Minister for Propaganda, Goebbels

Activity

1   Create a timeline to show the main developments in relations between Austria and Germany, 1919 to 1938.

2   There were a number of reasons why the British government accepted the *Anschluss*. Working with a partner, write down as many as you can using bullet points. There is no need to explain them fully at this stage.

3   Now try to group your reasons together into different categories. For instance, you may have several which arise out of the widespread belief that the Paris Peace Settlement (1919) had treated both Austria and Germany unfairly.

4   Finally, present your findings in the form of a spider diagram: Why did the British government accept the *Anschluss*? Try to make your diagram as analytical as possible. If you have access to a flip chart, present your findings to the rest of the class.

Source question practice

Source A

It was evident that (in March 1938) deeply as both (France and Britain) resented Hitler's brutal action, neither the British nor the French people were prepared to go to war to prevent German Austria from becoming a part of the German Reich. Indeed, there were many who believed that Austria, in the truncated form to which it had been reduced by the Treaty of Versailles, could not exist as an independent state.… In February and March of 1938 there was no chance of stopping Hitler except by war or by a threat of war, and neither we nor the French were prepared to fight what was claimed to be the unification of the German people. The result as far as Hitler was concerned was the winning of a strategic position in readiness for a move against Czechoslovakia.

From the memoirs of Lord Templewood (Sir Samuel Hoare), *Nine Troubled Years*, published in 1954. Hoare was Home Secretary in Chamberlain's cabinet at the time of *Anschluss*.

1   How useful is **Source A** in explaining the British reaction to *Anschluss*?

In reaching a conclusion you should refer to:

○   *the origin and possible purpose of the source*

○   *the content of the source*

○   *recalled knowledge.*

Anschluss: the annexation of Austria

Source B

The big question which all Germans asked themselves was, 'What will England do?' England, however, left it to words to carry conviction, as Hitler on 10th March had undoubtedly foreseen. Nor indeed were Her Majesty's Government in a position to save Austria by their actions. The case against Hitler was not yet a cast-iron one. Austria was German, and many Austrians were whole-heartedly in favour of union with the Reich. The love of the British public for peace was too great for it to approve of a war in respect of which the moral issue was in possible doubt.

From *Failure of a Mission*, by Nevile Henderson, the British Ambassador in Berlin between 1937 and 1939.

2 How far do you agree with the analysis of the British government's response to *Anschluss*, given in **Source B**?

Use the source and recalled knowledge.

10 Crisis over Czechoslovakia

Introduction

After the success of the Anschluss, it was clear to many observers that Czechoslovakia would be Hitler's next target. Czechoslovakia was vitally important to the balance of power in Europe. Now that the League of Nations was losing credibility after its failure over Abyssinia, a workable system of alliances was the one thing which could save Czechoslovakia from German aggression. A German takeover would inevitably mean that Hitler would dominate the continent of Europe. This nightmare scenario was the last thing the British and French governments wanted. As a historian of the period states:

> To France in particular the friendly democracy of Czechoslovakia was the one element in her post-war alliances which remained trustworthy... France, therefore,... must be expected to intervene for the defence of Czechoslovakian integrity... it seemed therefore a vital interest of Great Britain, as a country involved in the fate of France, as a country threatened by a Germany dominating Europe and reinforced by the products and munitions of Bohemia [a reference to the Skoda armaments works in Brno], and as a country desirous of peace, to do her best to ensure that no attack on Czechoslovakian independence took place... Since it was generally assumed that the Czechs themselves would not surrender without a struggle, any attack upon their country entailed the overwhelming probability of a general war.
>
> GM Gathorne-Hardy, A Short History of International Affairs 1920–1939, 4th edition, 1950

The Czechoslovak context

Czechoslovakia had been established at the end of World War One. The Czechs and Slovaks had been subjects of the Austro–Hungarian empire until then, but under the energetic leadership of Tomas Masaryk had forged an independent, democratic state, recognised by the Allies even before the Versailles Peace Conference. The Czechoslovaks were keen

Source 10.1

Central Europe, 1919–1938

Legend:
- Borders 1919–1939
- Germany border after Anschluss, March 1938

Ethnic groups
- Czechs
- Slovaks
- Ukrainians
- Others
- Germans
- Hungarians
- Poles

supporters of the League of Nations and had military alliances with France and the Soviet Union.

They had a well-equipped army, a modern armaments industry based on the huge Skoda works in Brno, and strong border defences. The president since the death of Masaryk in 1935 was the former Foreign Minister, Edvard Benes, 'a sure-footed democrat and negotiator with a fine instinct for compromise' (Ronald Cameron, *Appeasement and the Road to War*, 1991).

However, this stable and prosperous country contained several ethnic minorities. In some ways Czechoslovakia resembled the Austro–Hungarian empire it replaced.

The Czechs were in the majority, but could only rule effectively with the Slovaks. Although their languages were similar, the Slovaks had an identity distinct from the Czechs. They had been under Hungarian rule before 1918, and many wanted some form of home rule or autonomy. The Slovaks were a traditional peasant people who resented the fact that most government jobs went to the better-educated Czechs. The Hungarians in southern Slovakia and the Poles in Teschen both hoped for reunification with their mother countries, while the Ukrainians of Ruthenia made similar demands to the Slovaks.

Edvard Benes (1884–1948). Son of a farmer, studied law before becoming a professor of sociology. Exiled during World War One, he played a key role along with Tomas Masaryk in the founding of Czechoslovakia. He was Foreign Minister from 1918–1935, briefly Prime Minister in 1921–22, and became President in 1935. Following the Munich agreement, he resigned and later set up a government-in-exile, first in France then, after 1940, in Britain. Benes returned to Czechoslovakia following liberation in 1945, and was re-elected President in 1946. He resigned after the Communist takeover in 1948 and died later that year.

The most numerous minority were the 3.5 million Germans, who lived mainly near the border with Germany, in an area known as the Sudetenland. Although they were far from being oppressed, they had been the ruling group in the old Austro–Hungarian empire and resented Czech domination. Some had lost property when the government carried out an extensive land reform. Although there was some acceptance of the new state in the mid and late 1920s, shown by German parties joining in government coalitions, the economic depression changed the situation again. German-speaking areas suffered high unemployment, as most of their industries were export-led. Employment in the Czech districts tended to be either in the growing armaments sector or small- and medium-sized enterprises catering for local markets inside Czechoslovakia.

Source 10.2

Ethnic composition of Czechoslovakia (1930)

Czechs	7,447,000
Germans	3,231,600
Slovaks	2,309,000
Hungarians	691,000
Ukrainians	549,000
Poles	81,700

Source: G.M. Gathorne-Hardy: *A Short History of International Affairs 1920–1939*, p463, Fourth Edition, 1950)

Konrad Henlein (1898–1945). Worked as a bank clerk and then as a PE teacher before leading the Sudeten German Party to a sweeping victory in the German-speaking areas of Czechoslovakia at the 1935 elections. Met Hitler several times in 1938 to receive instructions on fomenting agitation and disruption in Czechoslovakia. He was appointed Gauleiter of Sudetenland in 1938 and later was Civil Commissioner in Bohemia and Moravia from 1939–1945. Captured by US forces in 1945, he committed suicide.

Nazi influence was great among the Sudeten Germans, as they were called. From 1933, a Sudeten German party had been established under Konrad Henlein, an ex-PE teacher. Playing on grievances which were mainly caused by high unemployment, Henlein's party demanded self-government and were encouraged, and indeed subsidised, by Nazi Germany. By 1937, they were by far the largest political group among the German minority.

By the standards of the period, Czechoslovakia did not oppress its minorities, but as a historian of Versailles, Margaret Macmillan, states:

> "
> *In districts with significant numbers of Germans, they could use their own language for official matters. There were German schools, universities, newspapers. But Czechoslovakia was still a Slav state. Its banknotes showed young women dressed in folkloric Czech or Slovak costumes. Germans... never felt they entirely belonged... At Munich in 1938 the Sudeten Germans provided [Hitler] with the excuse to destroy Czechoslovakia.*
>
> Margaret Macmillan, *Peacemakers*, 2002

Hitler's aims

From his early days in pre-1914 Vienna, Hitler had always hated the Czechs. His racist beliefs led him to believe that Czechs were part of the sub-human Slav group of nations. As a democratic state emerging from the Versailles settlement of 1919, Czechoslovakia was a particular object for Hitler's venom.

In the Hossbach Memorandum (see Chapter 9), Hitler clearly stated the necessity of destroying Austria and Czechoslovakia before facing a possible conflict with the west. Therefore, he would not be satisfied with either autonomy for the Sudeten Germans within Czechoslovakia or the transfer of the area to Germany. Hitler made it clear to his generals that he wanted war, even at the risk of Britain and France being involved, although he was cagey about an exact timetable. Since the reoccupation of the Rhineland (see Chapter 5), effective French help for Czechoslovakia would be difficult, especially as Germany started to construct the Westwall or Siegfried Line in 1938 – a line of fortifications along the German–French border. Hitler gave support to Henlein to enable him to weaken Czechoslovakia from within, while Propaganda Minister Josef Goebbels orchestrated a media onslaught against the Czechs, accusing them of atrocities against the Sudeten Germans.

While there were a number of generals and top officials in Germany who were worried about the risk of war, especially against Britain and France, they were quite happy at the prospect of Czechoslovakia being destroyed. Events moved mostly in Hitler's favour throughout the period of the Czech crisis.

The British view

Chamberlain began to take much more personal control of foreign policy than his predecessor, Stanley Baldwin. The resignation of Eden as Foreign Secretary in February 1938 (see previous chapter) gave him the opportunity. A new, more active policy was suggested by the new Foreign Secretary, Lord Halifax, in a policy statement to the French government soon after the *Anschluss*. First he described how the situation had changed:

> *It is undeniable that the military position of Czechoslovakia has been seriously weakened by the incorporation of Austria in the Reich. The absence of fortifications along the former Czechoslovak–Austrian border lays the heart of Czechoslovakia open to German attack. There is little hope, therefore, that military operations against Germany by… France and the Soviet Union, could be made effective in time to prevent the military occupation of Czechoslovakia if and when Germany decided to make an attack upon her.*
>
> *EL Woodward, Documents on British Foreign Policy 1919–1939, 3rd series*

Halifax then concluded by saying that the British and French governments should try to settle the questions involving the German minority within the integrity of the Czechoslovak state. Chamberlain was blunter still in his diary:

> " We could not help Czechoslovakia – she would simply be a pretext for going to war with Germany… I have therefore abandoned the idea of giving guarantees to Czechoslovakia, or the French in connection with her obligations to that country.
>
> *K Feiling: The Life of Neville Chamberlain, 1946*

When the crisis blew up later in the year, Chamberlain would take a much more proactive approach than in the previous crises over the Rhineland and Austria.

Lord Halifax (1881–1959). Born Edward Frederick Linley Wood, he was a Conservative MP from 1910–1925. Created Baron Irwin in 1925, he was Viceroy of India from 1926–31. He was appointed Foreign Secretary on Eden's resignation in 1938, and so is closely associated with Chamberlain's appeasement policies. Served as Ambassador to the USA from 1941–46.

The crisis unfolds

On February 20 1938, before the *Anschluss*, Hitler promised protection to German minorities outside the Reich. This was a clear signal of his intentions. Despite his assurance to the Czechoslovak government the day after his annexation of Austria (14 March) that he wished to improve German–Czech relations, few people were fooled. On the same day, France and the Soviet Union declared that they would honour their treaty obligations to aid Czechoslovakia if it was attacked.

Litvinov, the Soviet Foreign Minister, proposed united action among the powers to stop further aggression. However, these proposals were rejected by Chamberlain in the House of Commons on 24 March.

On 24 April, Henlein announced an eight-point programme of demands in a speech at Karlsbad. The so-called 'Karlsbad Decrees' included:

- full equality of status for Germans
- full autonomy for German areas
- freedom for Germans to adhere to 'the ideology of Germans'.

Henlein was doing his duty to Hitler in cranking up the pressure on the Czech government. As he said later, 'we must always demand so much that we cannot be satisfied'. The Czech government rejected the Karlsbad decrees.

A few days later, Henlein visited London and Berlin. On his return, disorder began to break out in German areas.

At the end of the month, Chamberlain and Halifax met their French counterparts in London, and agreed to use their influence to bring about a peaceful solution to the Sudeten German question. This resulted in pressure being brought to bear on the Czechs to make more concessions to the Sudeten Germans.

However, there is evidence that Hitler was not in any hurry to solve the Czech problem, as shown by this interim draft of Case Green (the secret code for invading Czechoslovakia) to his generals on 20 May:

> It is not my intention to smash Czechoslovakia by military action in the immediate future without provocation, unless an unavoidable development of the political conditions within Czechoslovakia forces the issue, or political events in Europe create a particularly favourable opportunity which may perhaps never recur.
>
> Quoted in J Noakes & G Pridham, Nazism 1919–1945, vol.3: Foreign Policy, War and Racial Extermination, 1988

Hitler got his 'favourable opportunity' much sooner than he imagined.

The May Crisis

Around 20–21 May, just before local elections were to be held in Czechoslovakia, rumours of German troop movements near the border led the Czech government to order partial mobilisation. Two Sudeten Germans were shot dead while trying to pass a frontier post without stopping after being challenged by border guards. The rumours of troop movements proved to be untrue, but gave President Benes an opportunity to test how much support he could rely on from his allies.

France and Britain made strong statements in favour of the Czechs, and the elections passed off without any trouble. It seemed that a potentially serious situation had been narrowly avoided by a firm line from the Czechs and their allies.

However, the most important consequence of the May Crisis was that Hitler was outraged by the false rumours, and at the perception that he had seemed to give in to pressure from the British and French. On 28 May, he asked his generals to revise 'Case Green' with a deadline to attack Czechoslovakia on 1 October 1938, saying, 'I am now utterly determined that Czechoslovakia should disappear from the map'.

Another important effect of the May Crisis was that Britain and France resented the fact (or so they believed) that the crisis had been manufactured by the Czechs. They felt they had been brought to the brink of war unnecessarily. Chamberlain in particular was clearer than ever that there would have to be a negotiated solution to the Sudeten German problem and that the Czechs would have to make concessions.

Throughout June and July, negotiations continued between the Sudeten German leaders and the Czechoslovak government, but any proposals failed to satisfy Henlein, so no progress was made.

Dr Goebbels made a 'helpful' speech on 21 June:

> *We will not look on much longer while 3,500,000 Germans are maltreated. We saw in Austria that one race cannot be separated into two countries, and we shall soon see it somewhere else.*

The Runciman Mission

Chamberlain decided that negotiations between the Czechoslovaks and the Sudeten Germans could be kept alive by despatching Lord Runciman to investigate the problem and mediate between the two sides. Walter Runciman was a businessman and Liberal leader in the House of Lords but had no diplomatic experience, and few really believed that he was genuinely independent of the British government. A contemporary observer noted:

> *Everyone knew, including Chamberlain, that Runciman's mission to 'mediate'... was impossible and absurd. They knew that Henlein... was not a free agent and could not negotiate, and that the dispute was now between Prague and Berlin... the Czechs knew perfectly well that Runciman had been sent by Chamberlain to pave the way for the handing over of the Sudetenland to Hitler. It was a shabby diplomatic trick.*
>
> William L Shirer, The Rise and Fall of the Third Reich, 1960

During his time in Czechoslovakia (August to September), Runciman became more sympathetic to the demands of the Sudeten Germans. He

spent about a month in negotiations with the two sides, but achieved little. President Benes was prepared to offer self-government to the Sudeten Germans and prepared a 'Nationalities Statute' which went as far as possible in satisfying the grievances of minorities without compromising on national security. Further concessions such as the 'fourth plan' which provided that all nationalities would share government jobs proportionately were also unacceptable to the Hitler-directed Sudeten Germans, even though they incorporated ali of the Henlein's Karlsbad Decrees of 24 April! One of the Sudeten leaders is said to have exclaimed, 'My God, they have given us everything!' (William L Shirer, *The Rise and Fall of the Third Reich*, 1960).

The next day (7 September), the Sudeten Germans broke off negotiations, using the excuse of Czech police violence against a Sudeten German MP. Several days of violence followed in Sudeten areas. Speaking at a Nazi Party rally in Nuremberg, Hitler further inflamed anti-Czech feelings:

> "
>
> *Czechoslovakia… is a democratic State, founded on democratic lines by forcing other nationalities without asking them into a structure manufactured by Versailles… Among these nationalities being suppressed in this State are 3,500,000 Germans… These Germans are creatures of God… The misery of the Sudeten Germans is without end. They [the Czechs] want to annihilate them. They are being oppressed in an inhuman and intolerable manner and treated in an undignified way… if these tortured creatures cannot obtain rights and assistance by themselves they can obtain both from us….*
>
> *…What the Germans demand is the right of self-determination which every other nation possesses… If the democracies [ie Britain and France], however, should be convinced that they must in this case protect with all their means the oppressors of the Germans, then this will have grave consequences.*
>
> *Adolf Hitler, 12 September 1938*

The speech had the desired effect. The sense of crisis was heightened. Two days of serious fighting in the Sudetenland followed, only quelled when the Czech government declared martial law and sent in troops to restore order. Henlein crossed the border to Germany to declare that the only solution was to grant all the Sudeten areas to Germany. Meanwhile, Lord Runciman decided that his function as a mediator was over. It appeared that the Runciman Mission had failed and that war was inevitable. It was now that Chamberlain decided to intervene personally.

Activity

1 Describe the strengths and weaknesses of Czechoslovakia in 1938.

2 In what ways did the May Crisis change Hitler's intentions towards Czechoslovakia?

3 How did British policy change as a result of the May Crisis?

Source question practice

Source A

A letter from Neville Chamberlain to King George VI, 13 September 1938

The continued state of tension in Europe which has caused such grave concern throughout the world has in no way been relieved, and in some ways has been aggravated by the speech delivered at Nuremberg last night by Herr Hitler. Your Majesty's Ministers are examining the position in the light of his speech, and with the firm desire to ensure, if this is at all possible, that peace may be restored.

On the one hand, reports are daily received in great numbers∴ that Herr Hitler has made up his mind to attack Czechoslovakia and then to proceed further East. He is convinced that the operation can be effected so rapidly that it will all be over before France or Great Britain could move.

On the other hand, Your Majesty's representative in Berlin [Sir Nevile Henderson, British Ambassador to Germany] has steadily maintained that Herr Hitler has not yet made up his mind to violence. He means to have a solution soon – this month – and if that solution… can be obtained peacefully, well and good. If not, he is ready to march.

In these circumstances, I have been considering the possibility of a sudden and dramatic step which might change the whole situation. The plan is that I should inform Herr Hitler that I propose at once to go over to Germany to see him. If he assents, and it would be difficult for him to refuse, I should hope to persuade him that he had an unequalled opportunity of raising his own prestige and fulfilling what he has so often declared to be his aim, namely the establishment of an Anglo–German understanding, preceded by a settlement of the Czechoslovakian question.

Of course I should not be able to guarantee that Dr Benes would accept this solution, but I should undertake to put all possible pressure on him to do so. The Government of France have already said that they would accept any plan approved by Your Majesty's Government or by Lord Runciman.

1 How fully does **Source A** show the British government's attitude to the escalating crisis over Czechoslovakia?

Use the source and recalled knowledge.

11 Munich: triumph or tragedy?

Introduction

In this chapter, the events of September 1938 will be narrated and analysed in considerable detail. The Munich Conference and the other meetings which preceded it are the climax to the policy of appeasement. To understand all the issues relating to this is essential not only for your success in the examination, but also to comprehend one of the most dramatic and possibly tragic events in 20th century history.

The first meeting – Berchtesgaden

On the evening of 13 September, Hitler received the following urgent message from the British Prime Minister:

> *In view of the increasingly critical situation I propose to come over at once and see you with a view to trying to find a peaceful solution. I propose to come across by air and am ready to start tomorrow.*
>
> *Quoted in William L Shirer, The Rise and Fall of the Third Reich, 1960*

Chamberlain had only once travelled by air before, on a short excursion. At the time, it was considered very enterprising for a politician to attempt such an exhausting programme at the age of sixty-nine. In retrospect, Chamberlain was embarking on what was to become commonplace in late twentieth century international affairs – shuttle diplomacy.

Leaving Britain at dawn, Chamberlain's flight landed at Munich airport about noon on 15 September. The meeting was to take place at Hitler's mountain residence, the Berghof, near Berchtesgaden. This involved Chamberlain in a three-hour rail journey from Munich, during which German troop trains passed in the opposite direction, heading for the frontier with Czechoslovakia. Hitler did not even meet his guest at Berchtesgaden station, but only when he arrived at the Berghof itself.

The main sources for what happened at the Berchtesgaden meeting are from Hitler's interpreter, Schmidt, and Chamberlain's memory of the conversation. The British Ambassador had urged Chamberlain not to let

the German Foreign Minister, Ribbentrop, in on the meeting. Feeling snubbed, Ribbentrop did not give Chamberlain a written transcript of Schmidt's translation, as was the usual diplomatic protocol.

Proceedings began after 4pm with a long rant from Hitler about what he had done for the German people, and how hard he had worked for peace. The only remaining issue, he said, was that of the three million Germans living in the Sudetenland. According to Schmidt's notes, Hitler was determined to solve the question even at the risk of a world war – 'the rest of the world might do what it liked'. Then, Chamberlain interrupted Hitler's monologue by asking him what the point of the meeting was if he (Hitler) was already determined to use force. This was the kind of intervention which no German would have dared to make, but it was effective. Hitler calmed down a little and suggested that there might, indeed, be a peaceful way forward, if Britain would agree to the ceding of the Sudeten areas to Germany on the basis of the right of self-determination.

This was a crucial difference from previous assumptions. Czechoslovakia would have to give up the Sudetenland to Germany. This went beyond even Henlein's Karlsbad Decrees. However, Chamberlain was not shocked, but said that he could not commit himself without consulting his cabinet and the French government. Hitler promised that he would not order any military action until they met again. Chamberlain privately remarked a couple of days later:

> "
> In spite of the hardness and ruthlessness I thought I saw in his face, I got the impression that here was a man who could be relied upon when he had given his word.
>
> Quoted in Keith Feiling, The Life of Neville Chamberlain, 1946

So Czechoslovakia would have to abandon its frontier defences as a result of this decision, or fight alone. All that had to be decided were the mechanics of when and how they were to give up the Sudetenland to Germany.

While Chamberlain returned home for discussions in cabinet and with the French, Hitler continued with military preparations. Henlein, now operating from inside Germany, was given help to organise and arm the Sudeten Free Corps to stir up trouble with the Czechs. Each of the five invading German armies were given their jumping-off points, and commanding officers selected.

Hitler also pressured the Hungarian and Polish governments to stake their territorial claims to Czechoslovakia. Henlein urged the Slovaks to step up their demands for autonomy. The disintegration of Czechoslovakia was being prepared. As Shirer describes:

> *Egged on by Berlin, the Polish government on September 21 demanded of the Czechs a plebiscite in the Teschen district, where there was a large Polish minority, and moved troops to the frontier of the area. The Hungarian government followed suit. On that day, too, September 22, the Sudeten Free Corps, supported by German SS detachments, occupied the Czech frontier towns of Asch and Eger, which jutted into German territory.*
>
> William L Shirer, The Rise and Fall of the Third Reich, 1960

Over the next week, Chamberlain was able to get agreement to the proposed deal from the cabinet and the French government. As you have seen in previous chapters, the French would not act against Germany without British support. The absence of a proper military alliance with Britain troubled them, and the treaty with the Soviet Union signed in 1935 was highly controversial within France. The left-wing Popular Front government (see Chapter 6) had lost power earlier in the year. The new Prime Minister was Edouard Daladier and, together with the Foreign Minister Georges Bonnet, he played a key role in the events of September 1938. What Chamberlain was asking the French to do was to ignore their alliance with Czechoslovakia in order to avoid war. They agreed with Chamberlain on 18 September, that all territory with more than 50 per cent Sudeten Germans would be handed over to Germany.

The following day the proposals were presented to the Czechoslovak government in Prague by British and French representatives. Initially, they were rejected, but further pressure was applied to President Benes and his government. They were told in no uncertain terms that if the proposals were rejected, they would face the Germans on their own. The Czechs were also aware that their alliance with the Soviet Union only involved assisting the Czechs if France did the same – which France wasn't going to. Faced with these unpalatable facts, the Czech government accepted the plan on 21 September.

Chamberlain was now ready to take flight to Germany to confirm the agreement drawn up at Berchtesgaden.

The second meeting – Bad Godesberg

Bad Godesberg is a beautiful spa town on the river Rhine. This meeting place was much more convenient for Chamberlain compared to Hitler's mountain retreat in Bavaria. As far as the British were concerned, the meeting, held 22–23 September, was to work out the details of the transfer of territory from Czechoslovakia to Germany. Meeting at the Hotel

Source 11.1

Dreesen, Chamberlain opened by explaining at length how he had managed to win over the French and the Czechs. He said that he was now prepared to accept that the Sudetenland should be turned over to the Germans without a plebiscite. The revised border of Czechoslovakia would be guaranteed internationally against aggression. At this point, Hitler flatly rejected the Franco–British plan, to Chamberlain's utter amazement, and outlined an even more aggressive set of demands. The Sudetenland was to be occupied immediately and non-German speakers were only to be allowed to take a suitcase of belongings with them. Even although Hitler was being given nearly everything he wanted, he was not getting his war. It was to be military occupation or nothing – the Czechs must be humiliated.

The following day (23 September) there was no face-to-face contact between the two leaders until 10.30 in the evening, when Hitler outlined his timetable for military occupation. The Czechs were to begin to evacuate the Sudetenland on 26 September, and complete it by 28 September. It seemed that this was the end of any discussions until, at the very end, Hitler made one concession – he promised to delay military occupation by two days from 28 September to 1 October, to give Chamberlain time. As we now know, 1 October was the date of the planned invasion of Czechoslovakia anyway, so this was hardly a major climbdown.

It would appear that deadlock had been reached. Chamberlain flew home to try to get agreement to the new, even harsher terms. There was opposition to these in the cabinet from Duff Cooper, the First Lord of the Admiralty (Navy Minister) and even Lord Halifax was mildly critical. Preparations for war in Britain, Czechoslovakia and France began.

Hitler spoke at a Nazi Party rally in the Berlin Sportspalast on Monday 26 September. According to the American journalist William Shirer, who was there, Hitler was:

> 66
> *Shouting and shrieking in the worst paroxysm I had ever seen him in, he venomously hurled personal insults at 'Herr Benes', declared that the issue of war or peace was now up to the Czech President and that, in any case, he would have the Sudetenland by October 1.*
>
> William L Shirer, The Rise and Fall of the Third Reich, 1960

Although Hitler's speech was ecstatically received by the Nazi Party faithful, there was other evidence that the German population as a whole were less than enthusiastic at the prospect of war. The following day, a motorised division paraded through the streets of Berlin during the evening rush-hour, but was virtually ignored by the crowds. Shirer noted in his diary that the action of the Berliners was 'the most striking demonstration against the war I've ever seen.'

On the same day came other bad news for Hitler:

- The Romanian and Yugoslavian governments had informed the Hungarians that if Czechoslovakia was attacked by Hungary, they would move against them. Hitler did not want the war to spread to the Balkans.
- France had begun to mobilise. German estimates suggested the French would be able to deploy 65 divisions in less than a week, against only 12 German ones on the frontier (the rest of the German army was on the Czech border).
- Mussolini was making absolutely no preparations to tie down any French troops on the Franco–Italian border.
- Czech mobilisation was nearly complete. The Czechs, with a field army of 800,000, and the French together outnumbered the Germans by two to one.
- The British had ordered the Royal Navy to mobilise, and anti-aircraft measures were taken.

Early in the evening, Hitler sat down to dictate a letter to Chamberlain which hinted that it might still be worth Chamberlain's while to continue his peace efforts. Chamberlain shared his thoughts with the nation in a live radio broadcast:

Munich: triumph or tragedy?

> "
> *How horrible, fantastic, incredible it is that we should be digging trenches and trying on gas-masks because of a quarrel in a far-away country between people of whom we know nothing! I would not hesitate to pay even a third visit to Germany if I thought it would do any good.*
>
> *Armed conflict between nations is a nightmare to me; but if I were convinced that any nation had made up its mind to dominate the world by fear of its force, I should feel that it must be resisted. Under such a domination, life for people who believe in liberty would not be worth living; but war is a fearful thing, and we must be very clear, before we embark on it, that it is really the great issues that are at stake.*
>
> Neville Chamberlain, radio broadcast, 27 September 1938

The third meeting – the Munich Conference

The pressure was now building on Hitler to accept some kind of negotiated settlement. Chamberlain replied promptly to Hitler's letter, offering to come to Germany again 'to discuss arrangements for transfer [of the Sudetenland].' He suggested a conference also involving representatives of Czechoslovakia, France and Italy. At the same time, Chamberlain sent a telegram to the Italian dictator urging him to persuade Hitler to accept his plan.

All through the morning of 28 September there was intense diplomatic activity in Berlin. The French ambassador was in the middle of conveying to Hitler a similar message to Chamberlain's – why risk a European war when you can get what you want by negotiation? – when Hitler was told that the Italian ambassador was outside and wished to see him urgently. This was the decisive intervention of Mussolini, letting it be known through his ambassador that he was prepared to mediate on the Sudeten question. He also asked Hitler to postpone his planned mobilisation. Hitler replied, 'Tell the *Duce* I accept his proposal.'

The time was twelve noon. Hitler's ultimatum to Czechoslovakia was due to expire at 2pm. He was able to inform British ambassador Henderson at 12.15 that he had postponed mobilisation for twenty-four hours, and by the end of Henderson's audience the Italian ambassador interrupted again to tell Hitler that Mussolini had agreed to Chamberlain's proposals for a meeting of the four powers.

Meanwhile, in Britain, Chamberlain was getting towards the end of a detailed speech on the crisis to the House of Commons. Although he

explained that the situation had improved somewhat thanks to Mussolini's intervention, it still remained serious. The whole atmosphere was one of gloom and depression, when Chamberlain was passed a note from Lord Halifax. He continued, after reading the note:

> *I have something further to say to the House yet. I have now been informed by Herr Hitler that he invites me to meet him at Munich tomorrow morning. He has also invited Signor Mussolini and Monsieur Daladier. Signor Mussolini has accepted and I have no doubt Monsieur Daladier will accept. I need not say what my answer will be.*

At this point the House of Commons erupted, according to Shirer, 'with a mass hysteria without precedent in its long history.' War had been avoided – for the moment.

Early the next afternoon (29 September) the representatives of Britain, Germany, France and Italy met in the Fuhrerbrau, part of the Nazi Party headquarters in Munich. No representative of Czechoslovakia was present at the conference which decided the fate of their country.

The conference quickly got on with the business of arranging the details of the transfer of the Sudetenland to Germany. Mussolini tabled a written proposal which provided the basis for the final settlement. This 'compromise

Source 11.2

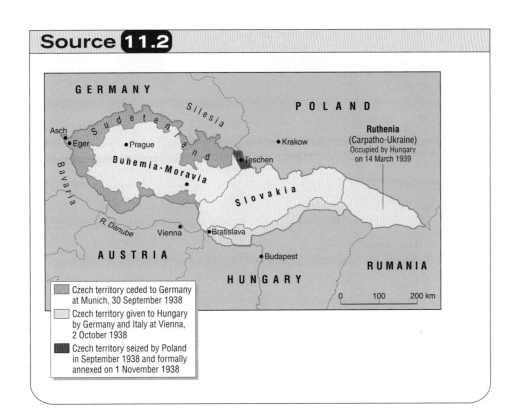

Czech territory ceded to Germany at Munich, 30 September 1938

Czech territory given to Hungary by Germany and Italy at Vienna, 2 October 1938

Czech territory seized by Poland in September 1938 and formally annexed on 1 November 1938

plan' had largely been drafted the day before by Göring and the German Foreign Office (bypassing the pro-war Foreign Minister, Ribbentrop) and approved by Hitler before being sent to Mussolini via the Italian ambassador. All this was unknown to the British and French delegations. The terms were similar to those discussed at Bad Godesberg (the second meeting), with a timetable for German occupation to be completed by 10 October. Two Czech representatives, waiting in an adjoining room, were officially informed of the decision by Chamberlain's adviser at 10pm. They now knew that they had no choice. Their allies had abandoned them. At 1am on 30 September, the four leaders signed the document known ever since as the Munich agreement. The German army would occupy the Sudetenland in four stages, from 1 October to 10 October. The Czechs were to leave all installations untouched. An International Commission was to arrange for plebiscites to be held in ethnically-mixed areas, and the new borders of Czechoslovakia, subject to the claims of the Hungarian and Polish minorities, would be guaranteed by Britain, France, Germany and Italy.

The next morning, Chamberlain called on Hitler in his private apartment with a further proposal. He had suggested this meeting during a break in the conference proceedings the previous day. Towards the end of their conversation, Chamberlain pulled a sheet of paper from his pocket and

Source 11.3

Neville Chamberlain, Adolf Hitler, Benito Mussolini and Hermann Göring stand together at the Munich Conference in 1938

asked Hitler if he would be prepared to sign. This was a joint declaration stating that both countries would continue to deal with problems by negotiation and resolved never to go to war with one another again. After reading it through, Hitler added his signature, although his interpreter recalled that he seemed reluctant. Chamberlain, on the other hand, was delighted.

On his return to Britain, at Heston airport, Chamberlain waved the document in the air with a great flourish in front of the waiting newsreel cameramen and journalists – perhaps an early example of news management by a government – and read out its contents. Later, huge crowds gathered outside 10 Downing Street, singing 'For He's a Jolly Good Fellow.' Speaking from a second floor window, Chamberlain spoke a few words. Referring to an earlier agreement made in Germany in 1878, he said:

> "
> *This is the second time in our history that there has come back from Germany to Downing Street peace with honour. I believe it is peace in our time.*

The feelings of relief and joy in Britain in the aftermath of Munich seemed apparent everywhere. Chamberlain received over 20,000 letters and telegrams of congratulation in the days following Munich.

Source 11.4

A German postcard from December 1938 showing the Sudetenland invaded by Nazi Germany

However, it must be remembered that there was considerable news management of the entire Czech crisis by the British government. BBC radio and cinema newsreels gave no alternative views or indication of the pressure which was put on the Czechs. Most newspapers supported appeasement. Opinion polls, as previously mentioned, were in their infancy in the 1930s. The evidence there is suggests that most people had very little knowledge of the issues at stake and many, perhaps even a majority, did not believe that the Munich settlement had brought a lasting peace.

The debate

It is important to distinguish between the arguments over Munich at the time and the historical debate, although there are obviously connections. Apart from the politicians, nobody at the time had access to some of the information on which decisions were made, whereas historians gained access to official documents in the 1960s, when the government allowed previously classified documents to be released after 30 years, rather than 50, as before. These have enhanced our understanding of the appeasement policy, although the arguments continue.

The Times was then the most influential newspaper in Britain, read by most of the people who might be described as the governing classes – politicians, top civil servants and businessmen. The editor, Geoffrey Dawson, was an enthusiastic supporter of Chamberlain, as shown by this editorial, headed 'A New Dawn':

> "
> *No conqueror returning from a victory on the battlefield has come home adorned with nobler laurels than Mr Chamberlain from Munich yesterday… He has not only relegated an agonizing episode to the past; he has found for the nations a new hope for the future. The joint declaration made by Herr Hitler and Mr Chamberlain… shall henceforth govern the whole of their relationships… By inserting a specific reference to the Anglo–German Naval Agreement, as well as to the negotiations so happily concluded at Munich, the Fuhrer reminds us of an earnest of his good intentions, which the British people, in the new atmosphere, will readily acknowledge.*
>
> The Times editorial, October 1, 1938

On 4 October, there was a full-scale debate on the Munich agreement in the House of Commons. Chamberlain was keen to portray the agreement as a triumph for appeasement, because Hitler's demands had been settled peacefully:

> *The real triumph is that it has shown that representatives of the four great powers can find it possible to agree a way of carrying out a difficult and delicate operation by discussion instead of by force of arms…*
>
> *The path which leads to appeasement is long and bristles with obstacles. The question of Czechoslovakia is the latest and perhaps the most dangerous. Now that we have got past it, I feel that it may be possible to make further progress along the road to sanity.*

A few Conservatives disagreed. Duff Cooper resigned from the government in protest and backbenchers such as Leo Amery and Winston Churchill spoke powerfully against the agreement, but the huge government majority was never in danger. The Labour and Liberal parties both opposed the agreement. Clement Attlee, leader of the Labour Party, spoke as follows:

> *We have been unable to go in for carefree rejoicing. We have felt that we are in the midst of a tragedy. We have felt humiliation. This has not been a victory for reason and humanity. It has been a victory for brute force… We have seen today a gallant, civilised and democratic people betrayed and handed over to a ruthless despotism.*

It seems that opinion in Britain was divided between those who felt relief that war had been avoided and others, like Attlee, who believed that the conflict had merely been postponed at the expense of the independence of a small democratic country.

With the benefit of hindsight, we can begin to explore the arguments for and against. What follows can only briefly summarise these, which contain points with which you will be familiar from earlier chapters. Much of the evidence, remember, only became publicly available decades later.

Arguments for the Munich agreement

Historical

Munich was the culmination of the policy of appeasement dating right back to 1919 (see Chapter 2). It was not something developed especially for Munich. In the words of historian AJP Taylor, 'it was a triumph for all that was best and most enlightened in British life; a triumph for those who had preached equal justice between people; a triumph for those who had courageously denounced the harshness and short-sightedness of Versailles.'

Military

There was still a lack of confidence in British defences in 1938. As already mentioned in Chapters 5 and 7, the government was aware that Britain's defence requirements had already been overstretched and could be again. Although spending had increased considerably by 1938, especially on air defence, the feeling was that the country was still vulnerable to attack from the air. Recent evidence from both China and Spain showed the full horrors of air bombardment, which seemed to bear out former Prime Minister Baldwin's gloomy prediction of 1932 that 'the bomber will always get through.' Although new aircraft such as the Hurricane and Spitfire fighters and the new radar system were being developed at this time, neither the aircraft nor the radar devices were available in sufficient numbers in 1938.

The army had been poorly equipped for years and was only just beginning to receive modern equipment and training in 1938. Only the navy seemed to be ready to fight, with modern ships such as aircraft carriers.

It has been argued, therefore, that a year later in September 1939, Britain was much readier for war than at Munich. Evidence to support this is that by September 1939 there were 26 fighter squadrons, as opposed to 6 the year before, and radar defences covering the entire south and east coasts of Britain, compared to 1938 when only the direct air routes to London were covered by radar. The arguments here are inconclusive, as Chamberlain was well aware of the facts and figures, and knew that the money for defence had been allocated well before September 1938.

British public opinion

As shown earlier in the chapter, while opinions about Munich differed, there seems little doubt that Chamberlain reflected what many British people felt – that another war would bring about unimaginable catastrophe, even worse than 1914–18. Therefore, it was better to sacrifice Czechoslovakia than risk plunging Europe into slaughter again.

Distrust of France

Mutual lack of confidence between Britain and France had already been seen over the Rhineland (see Chapter 5) and the Spanish Civil War (see Chapter 6). Over Czechoslovakia it was clear that France would only move against Germany with British support, and this was not forthcoming. French public opinion was much more divided than Britain and successive governments pinned their military strategy on the Maginot Line, which by its very nature precluded any real offensive operations.

Suspicion of the Soviet Union

At the time, and later, Chamberlain was criticised for failing to involve the Soviet Union in the crisis. After all, Czechoslovakia had an alliance with the

Soviets. Faced with the combined might of Britain, France, Czechoslovakia and the Soviet Union, Hitler would surely have backed down. However, Soviet troops could only get access to Czechoslovakia through Poland or Romania, as they did not have a common border, and neither country was prepared to admit them. It should also be remembered that the Red Amy was in the midst of a massive purge of its high-ranking officers, which did little to inspire confidence in its ability to fight a major war.

Attitude of the British Dominions

As mentioned in Chapter 5, the self-governing dominions had shown in 1937 that they would not automatically support Britain in a European war. This had been reinforced in September 1938 when the High Commissioners (ambassadors) of Australia, Canada and South Africa made it clear that they were not prepared to go to war over Czechoslovakia.

Was Czechoslovakia worth fighting for?

Chamberlain had made his attitude clear to the British public in his radio broadcast of 27 September. He felt that Benes should have made concessions to the Sudeten Germans before the crisis began. There were also those who questioned the viability of the Czechoslovak state, containing as many minority groups as it did (see Chapter 8).

Arguments against Munich

Morality

Czechoslovakia was not even allowed to attend the conference at which it was effectively partitioned. This was as much a diktat as Versailles was to Germany.

Military

It now seems clear that Hitler would have had a very difficult fight on his hands if Britain and France had stood by Czechoslovakia. With most of Hitler's forces concentrated to attack the Czechs, the French would have had overwhelming numerical superiority in the west, both in the air and on the ground. The Czech army was large and well-equipped and would have fought well from its strong defences in northern Bohemia.

Diplomatic

Hitler was disappointed not to have his war in September 1938. Appeasement had not worked in the way Chamberlain hoped. Hitler saw Munich as a humiliating climbdown and within a month of the agreement he was ordering his generals to make plans to invade the rest of Czechoslovakia. He did not care what Britain or France might do now –

'Next time he was determined he would not be blocked by last-minute diplomatic manoeuvres of the western powers, whose weakness he had seen with his own eyes at Munich.' (Ian Kershaw, *Hitler 1936–1945: Nemesis*, 2001.)

Activity

1   Examine carefully all the arguments made for the Munich agreement. Create a spider diagram with a brief outline of each argument.

2   Looking at your diagram, which argument seems, in your opinion, to be:

   (a) the most convincing
   (b) the least convincing?

   Give reasons for your choices.

3   'It is much easier to argue against the Munich agreement with the benefit of hindsight.'

   How far do you agree with this statement? Justify your answer.

Source question practice

Source A

In the Czech affair… the British took the initiative. Chamberlain tried to get ahead of events, instead of waiting for them to happen. He did not act alone. Policy was conducted by the foreign secretary (Halifax) and the foreign office until Chamberlain intervened in the middle of September… It was British policy in the fullest sense. Its object was to extract from the Czechoslovak government concessions which would satisfy the German inhabitants before Hitler imposed a solution by force.

From AJP Taylor, *English History 1914–1945*, 1965

Source B

By his courage and perseverance, Mr Neville Chamberlain stands out clear above all others as the man who saved the peace of the world. His return to London last evening from the fateful conference at Munich was in the nature of a triumph. The cheers of the large crowds which assembled to greet him were the vocal expression of the heartfelt relief of nearly all the people of Britain…

What is most important is the fact that he has been successful in preserving the peace and preventing the slaughter of thousands, perhaps millions of people, none of whom desires war. Blessed be our Prime Minister, and blessed be the little country of Czechoslovakia which helped by its self-sacrifice to ensure that peace.

Mr Chamberlain has brought home with him a document signed by Herr Hitler and himself binding Germany and Great Britain to settle all problems by the method of consultation, and not by force. Surely we may rest our minds that the German Fuhrer will acknowledge a pact which will go far to ensure the future peace of Europe.

The Perthshire Advertiser, 1 October 1938

Source C

All is over. Silent, mournful, abandoned, broken, Czechoslovakia recedes into the darkness. She has suffered in every respect by her association with the Western democracies and with the League of Nations, of which she has always been an obedient servant... I do not grudge our loyal, brave people, who were ready to do their duty no matter what the cost, who never flinched under the strain of last week – I do not grudge them the natural, spontaneous outburst of joy and relief when they learned that the hard ordeal would no longer be required of them at the moment; but they should know the truth.

They should know that there has been gross neglect and deficiency in our defences; they should know that we have sustained a defeat without a war, the consequences of which will travel with us along our road; they should know that we have passed an awful milestone in our history, when the whole equilibrium of Europe has been deranged... This is only the beginning of the reckoning. This is only the first sip, the first foretaste of a bitter cup which will be proffered to us year by year unless, by a supreme recovery of vigour, we rise again and take our stand for freedom as in the olden time.

From a speech by Winston Churchill in the House of Commons, 5 October 1938

1 How fully does **Source A** explain British policy during the Munich crisis?

   Use the source and recalled knowledge.

2 Compare the views in **Sources B** and **C** about the Munich agreement.

   Compare the sources overall and in detail.

Munich: triumph or tragedy?

The consequences of Munich

Britain

In Britain, public delight about Munich was short-lived. Chamberlain, however, remained upbeat, and saw the Anglo–German declaration leading to a comprehensive settlement of European problems. In the British cabinet, some ministers disagreed, seeing Munich as simply providing the country with breathing space. An acceleration of the rearmament programme, supported by the service chiefs, was demanded and agreed. The defence budget increased from £1.5 billion in 1938 to £2.1 billion in 1939, most of this increase going on fighter aircraft.

Source 12.1

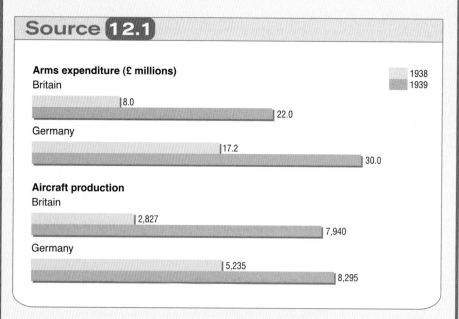

Arms expenditure (£ millions)

	1938	1939
Britain	8.0	22.0
Germany	17.2	30.0

Aircraft production

	1938	1939
Britain	2,827	7,940
Germany	5,235	8,295

Figures going back further reveal a steady increase in rearmament in Britain from 1936 onwards, but the acceleration after Munich is clear from the figures. However, the German figures also show a similar rise, although from a higher starting point.

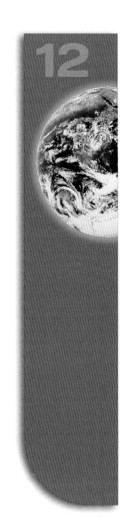

The British people seemed agreed that in the immediate future there should be, in the words of one historian 'an unrelaxing and energetic concentration on the needs of national defence' (GM Gathorne-Hardy, *A Short History of International Affairs 1920–1939*, 4th edition, 1950). A poem published in the humorous magazine Punch on 12 October 1938 reflected the mood of the nation:

> "
> *It's peace!*
> *The gas-masks are distributed.*
> *It's peace!*
> *Ten millions are contributed.*
> *We've dug up lots of trenches in everybody's garden,*
> *We've commandeered the underground without your leave or pardon;*
> *Father's a balloon-barrage, mother's an air-warden.*
> *It's peace! It's peace!*
>
> Quoted in GM Gathorne-Hardy, A Short History of International
> Affairs 1920–1939, 4th edition, 1950

Czechoslovakia

President Benes and his government resigned at the time of the Munich agreement. The new government tried its best to appease the Germans by banning the Communist Party and passing anti-Jewish legislation. The Slovaks and the Ukrainians were granted a substantial measure of autonomy, with their own parliaments and executives. Hungary and Poland were both granted territory by Hitler after Munich (see map in previous chapter).

Abandoned by its former allies, the rump Czechoslovakia had little room for manoeuvre. Its future depended on Hitler's plans.

France

Munich was a disaster for France. Militarily, the loss of Czechoslovakia and its thirty-five army divisions signalled the end of its system of military alliances in central and eastern Europe. These alliances had offset the potential – and now actual – military superiority of Germany. Daladier, the French Prime Minister, was under no illusions as to the what had happened. When told that there were large crowds waiting at the airport on his return from Munich, he thought it was a hostile anti-government demonstration against the agreement. He was surprised and relieved on touchdown to be met by cheers.

The consequences of Munich

The Soviet Union

Despite its military alliances with Czechoslovakia and France, the Soviet Union had at no time been consulted either before or during the Munich conference. Stalin did not forget this snub and from this time onwards he began to have doubts about the value of a pro-western foreign policy. This had direct and fateful consequences within less than a year of Munich.

Germany

As mentioned in the previous chapter, Hitler felt cheated by the Munich agreement. He still intended to smash what remained of Czechoslovakia. According to Ian Kershaw:

> *He was determined not to be hemmed in by the western powers. He was more than ever convinced that they would not have fought for Czechoslovakia, and that they would and could do nothing to prevent Germany extending its dominance in central and eastern Europe.*
>
> *Ian Kershaw, Hitler 1936–1945: Nemesis, 2001*

In the final analysis, Hitler did not care if further expansion led to war with the western powers – he must have the rest of Czechoslovakia.

Why did Hitler want to take over the rest of Czechoslovakia?

Hitler believed that he had been manoeuvred into a humiliating climb down at Munich. Just after the agreement, he was heard to say 'That fellow Chamberlain has spoiled my entry into Prague.'

Hitler had always hated the Czechs. This dated back to his youth in Austria.

Most of Czechoslovakia's considerable economic wealth remained outside German control. About 80 per cent of the engineering, machine tool and electrical industries lay within the new borders of rump Czechoslovakia.

The Czech armaments industry was by far the biggest in central and eastern Europe. Czech machine-guns, field-guns, and anti-aircraft guns were widely believed to be better than their German equivalents. All this and much more would fall into German hands with the takeover of the complex of Skoda factories in and around Brno in Moravia. It has been estimated that Hitler gained enough arms and equipment to outfit twenty army divisions.

The Czech gold and foreign currency reserves were considerable, and would help to relieve the strain on the German economy caused by the massive rearmament programme.

The strategic and geographical position of Czechoslovakia was the key to German expansion. As Kershaw notes, 'possession of the rectangular, mountain-rimmed territories of Bohemia and Moravia on the south-eastern edge of the Reich offered a recognizable platform for further eastward expansion and military domination.' In the event of any conflict with the western powers, Germany's eastern defences would be much stronger with the addition of the rest of Czechoslovakia. Germany would also be able to dominate the Balkans more readily.

Kristallnacht

Before any further moves took place, there was an event in Germany which shocked many outsiders and revealed the true nature of the Nazi government to them. On 7 November, Herschel Grynszpan, a seventeen-year-old Jewish refugee in France, shot dead a diplomat in the German Embassy in Paris. Within two days, the German government launched a night of anti-Jewish terror throughout Germany. Hundreds of Jewish-owned shops were set on fire and had their windows smashed – hence the name *Kristallnacht*, 'the night of the broken glass.' In total over 100 synagogues were burnt down, 8,000 shops destroyed, 30,000 Jews arrested and sent to concentration camps, and perhaps 100 murdered. The Jewish community was made to pay a collective fine of one billion marks.

World opinion was outraged by such open, state-ordered brutality. Chamberlain, under pressure from within his cabinet and from the churches and opposition politicians, conceded that any discussions with the Nazi government should be indefinitely postponed.

Hitler saw the international criticism of *Kristallnacht* as simply more evidence of a 'Jewish world conspiracy.'

Chamberlain persists with appeasement

Chamberlain was not easily deflected from his appeasement policies after Munich, despite *Kristallnacht*. In January 1939, he and Halifax visited Mussolini in Rome. Unaware of the real background to Mussolini's offer which led to the Munich conference, Chamberlain felt he could influence Mussolini to moderate any future demands which Hitler might have. Mussolini told him he would not be able to do this. Nevertheless, Chamberlain returned from Italy convinced that his policy was still on track for success.

However, faced with gloomy intelligence assessments about Hitler's intentions on his return, such as a possible assault on France, Chamberlain agreed to what amounted to a radical change in defence strategy. Plans for a greatly expanded British Expeditionary Force to be ready for despatch to France at short notice were agreed, and high-level military talks between Britain and France took place for the first time since the Great War.

The occupation of Czechoslovakia – the end of appeasement?

Despite promises at Munich, Germany had failed to give a guarantee of Czechoslovakia's independence. The reasons were obvious, as shown above. To speed the break-up of Czechoslovakia, the Germans encouraged separatist movements in Slovakia and Ruthenia. When the pro-German Czech government finally took action to quell disturbances by dismissing the autonomous governments in these areas and arresting several pro-independence Slovak ministers, the Germans were initially taken by surprise. They soon recovered and acted decisively, forcing the dismissal of the new Slovak government, and proclaiming its 'independence' on 14 March 1939.

Source 12.2

Geographers at the London geography institute George Philips & Sons Ltd. working on changes to maps of Europe in March 1939

The Czech president Hacha was invited to a meeting in Berlin that evening at which he was forced to sign away the independence of the remaining Czech provinces of Bohemia and Moravia. In the small hours of 15 March Hacha, after having previously fainted in the face of angry harangues by Hitler, Goering and Ribbentrop, telephoned Prague to order his government to surrender. At 6am, German troops crossed the revised borders into Bohemia and Moravia, meeting no resistance. In the evening, Hitler entered Prague in triumph, declaring 'the Protectorate of Bohemia and Moravia.' Simultaneously, Hungarian troops occupied and annexed Ruthenia. On 16 March, German troops entered Slovakia and two days later a treaty of 'protection' was signed with the new puppet government led by Father Tiso, a Catholic priest. The map of Europe had been redrawn again without a shot being fired. The Czech army remained in its barracks and surrendered its weapons to the occupying forces.

For the first time, Hitler had taken over territory which was not inhabited by Germans.

In the words of one historian:

> *The Nazi takeover of Czechoslovakia destroyed the Munich agreement, wounded Chamberlain's reputation and mortally wounded the policy of appeasement. It revealed that diplomatic agreements signed with the Nazi dictator were worthless. It was no longer credible to argue, as Chamberlain had done, that Hitler's foreign policy aims were exclusively linked to a revision of the Treaty of Versailles. On the contrary, it became generally accepted that Hitler fully intended to dominate Europe by military force unless he was halted.*
>
> Frank McDonough, *Neville Chamberlain, Appeasement and the British Road to War*, 1998.

In Britain, even the staunchly pro-appeasement Conservative MP Henry 'Chips' Cannon was outraged:

> *Hitler has entered Prague, apparently, and Czechoslovakia has ceased to exist. No balder, bolder departure from the written bond has ever been committed in history. The manner of it surpassed comprehension and his callous desertion of the Prime Minister is stupefying. I can never forgive him.*
>
> Henry 'Chips' Channon, diary entry, March 15 1939

While it is tempting to see the occupation of Czechoslovakia as the end of appeasement, things are not that simple. Although stepping up rearmament, as we have seen, Chamberlain continued to maintain his belief that war could still be avoided if Hitler was not provoked.

Events were once again to prove him wrong.

Activity

1 Look at **Source 12.1**. What happened to British defence spending after Munich and why?

2 What reasons are outlined for Hitler taking over the rest of Czechoslovakia. Which do you see as the most important one(s)? Justify your answer.

3 Why was the invasion of Czechoslovakia in March 1939 different from Hitler's previous foreign policy moves?

Source question practice

Source A

As a human tragedy, the extinction of the Czechoslovak republic transcends imagination. It is the first time that Hitler has invaded and conquered a country that is not 'German' in the 'racial' sense. He has again and again professed that he only wants only Germans in Germany and a 'racially' homogenous Reich. In his speech on September 26, he said, 'I do not want any Czechs.' He has now incorporated the entire Czech population in the Reich.

Was it necessary for him to occupy Prague? It was not, for the Czechs capitulated even before the supreme humiliation was inflicted. The reasons for the occupation lie in Hitler's own nature. He is a German romantic, and to him Prague is a city of romance, of ancient legend, and associated with Germany's distant past. He also hates the Czechs intensely, and has been impelled by the wish – very evident in his speeches for nearly a year – to humiliate them and crush them.

From the *Manchester Guardian*, March 16 1939

Source B

Is this the last attack upon a small state or is it to be followed by others? Is this, in effect, a step in the direction of an attempt to dominate the world by force?... While I am not prepared to engage this country in new and unspecified commitments operating under conditions which cannot now been foreseen, yet no greater mistake could be made than to suppose that because it believes war to be a senseless and cruel thing, this nation has so lost its fibre that it will not take part to the utmost of its power in resisting such a challenge if it were ever made.

From a speech by Neville Chamberlain in Birmingham on March 17 1939

1 Compare the views expressed in **Sources A** and **B** about the invasion of Czechoslovakia.

Compare the sources overall and in detail.

13 The Polish Crisis and the outbreak of World War Two

Introduction

It had been obvious from early 1939 that Hitler's next step would be Poland. This chapter examines the build up to the Polish crisis, Britain's failure to make an alliance with the Soviet Union, the bombshell of the Nazi–Soviet Pact and the actual outbreak of the war. Did Chamberlain still cling to the hope that Hitler could still be appeased over Poland and a full-scale war avoided? Or was this simply another illusion?

Poland between the wars

Poland had been re-established in 1919 at Versailles. Unlike Czechoslovakia it was not a new country and although it did contain a considerable number of ethnic minorities it was more ethnically united than Czechoslovakia. Nevertheless, the German population of the so-called Polish Corridor and Upper Silesia was a major potential flashpoint, especially after Hitler came to power. The status of the port of Danzig, with its almost wholly German population, was also an area of conflict, even before 1933. Danzig had been taken from Germany to fulfil the promise of ensuring that the state of Poland would have access to the sea. The Baltic coastline at this point had only one major port, that of Danzig, but the peacemakers felt it would be unjust to simply give it to Poland. So it was created a Free City under League of Nations administration in a customs union with Poland. The League commissioner was a very busy man, dealing with endless disputes between the Germans and the Poles.

These disputes became the heart of Hitler's case against Poland when he started to apply pressure on Poland after March 1939.

Poland's long-standing alliance with France had been weakened by the Non-Aggression Pact signed with Germany in 1934 (see Chapter 4), and the failures of French diplomacy in subsequent years left Poland dangerously isolated between Soviet Russia and Germany. This potentially serious situation was more apparent after the Munich agreement, given Britain and France's failure to defend the integrity of Czechoslovakia.

Source 13.1

Map legend:

— Poland, 1939
- - - International borders before 1939
— International borders after 1939

Ethnic groups

Czechs	Germans
Slovaks	Hungarians
Ukrainians	Poles
Russians	Lithuanians
Others	

Chamberlain's guarantee to Poland

On 23 March, a week after taking over the rest of Czechoslovakia, the Germans occupied the port of Memel in Lithuania. On 31 March, Chamberlain announced a guarantee of support to Poland, which was swiftly matched by a French guarantee to the Poles. Chamberlain explained the guarantee in a statement to parliament on 3 April:

> *I now have to inform the House that in the event of any action which clearly threatened Polish independence, and which the Polish government accordingly considered it vital to resist with their national force, His Majesty's Government would feel themselves bound at once to lend the Polish government all support in their power. They have given the Polish government an assurance to this effect.*

So, Chamberlain gave to Poland what he had refused Czechoslovakia even though there was little that Britain or France could do to defend Poland directly. The Polish armed forces were weaker than those of Czechoslovakia, and the country did not have any natural defensive barriers to invasion from the west, north or east. The guarantee also made no reference to defending Poland's existing borders, suggesting some ambiguity. On the face of it, the guarantee made no military sense. As Shirer commented:

> Chamberlain… had undertaken to unilaterally guarantee an Eastern country run by a junta of politically inept 'colonels' who up to this moment had closely collaborated with Hitler, who, like hyenas had joined the Germans in the carving up of Czechoslovakia and whose country had been rendered militarily indefensible by the very German conquests which Britain and Poland had helped the Reich to achieve.
>
> *William L Shirer, The Rise and Fall of the Third Reich, 1960*

Reasons for the Polish guarantee were complex and unclear. Was it to deter further German aggression in eastern Europe? Did Chamberlain believe he could deter Germany this way without provoking Hitler by making an alliance with the Soviet Union? Would a guarantee of support for Poland encourage Hitler to negotiate over Danzig?

The evidence suggests that Chamberlain was not ready to give up appeasement completely. If he was, Britain and France would surely have pushed for a full-scale anti-German alliance involving the Soviet Union.

Hitler's response

Hitler reacted firmly to Chamberlain's moves. On 1 April, speaking at the launch of the battleship *Tirpitz*, he strongly criticised the British for interfering and warned the Poles about their connections with the western powers. Two days later, Hitler ordered the army to draw up plans for an attack on Poland at any time from 1 September onwards. By the end of April, he had announced that he would no longer be bound by either the Anglo–German Naval Treaty of 1935, or the 1934 non-aggression pact with Poland.

Meanwhile, Mussolini invaded Albania on 7 April, indicating that Italy had no interest in any agreements with Britain or France. The *Duce* was now linking his future closely to his fellow-dictator. Britain and France responded by offering Polish-type guarantees to Romania, Greece and Turkey, which were accepted.

On 22 May, Hitler and Mussolini signed the Pact of Steel, a military alliance which made many observers feel that war was only a matter of time, although it is now known that Mussolini only signed reluctantly, making it clear that Italy was not ready for war. The evidence suggests that Hitler envisaged war with Poland only, and did not imagine that Britain or France would intervene to stop him. As Hitler said to his generals the day after the Pact of Steel was announced:

> *We are left with the decision: to attack Poland at the first suitable opportunity… There will be war… [but] it must not come to a simultaneous showdown with the West.*

He also made it clear that he would not be deterred by British and French intervention, but did not think it likely. Plans for the attack on Poland continued through the summer, but the diplomatic focus now switched to the Soviet Union.

The Nazi–Soviet Pact

By the end of May, Chamberlain authorised negotiations to start with the Soviet Union but he was less than enthusiastic about such an alliance with Russia. His hostility to communism was well-known, but in this he was no different from most Conservatives. He was also aware that the Russian army had been weakened by bitter and bloody internal rows which had left it militarily weak. He also knew that Poland was deeply suspicious of its neighbour Russia. But perhaps the most important reason for Chamberlain's reluctance was that he still felt his appeasement policy was right. He was not prepared to accept the logic of his opponents that only a full-scale anti-Nazi alliance would deter Hitler.

The negotiations proceeded slowly throughout the summer of 1939 and it is clear that the Soviets were frustrated by the slow response of the British and French to their proposals. As AJP Taylor stated:

> *The diplomatic exchanges show that delays came from the West and that the Soviet Government answered with almost breathtaking speed… If dates mean anything, the British were spinning things out, the Russians were anxious to conclude.*
>
> AJP Taylor, The Origins of the Second World War, 1961

By August little had happened. Chamberlain probably felt he could safely spin out the negotiations because Hitler and Stalin could never reach an agreement. Their ideologies were so hostile to each other that a pact was unthinkable. But Stalin's aim throughout was to avoid war at all costs and a short-term agreement with Germany now seemed a better option. On 23 August the unthinkable happened, and the Nazi–Soviet Pact was announced to a stunned world. The agreement consisted of a non-aggression pact, a trade agreement, and a secret protocol outlining the areas of influence in eastern Europe, including the division of Poland. However, nothing was certain except that if war against Poland did break out, the Soviet Union would be neutral.

Hitler's reasoning for the agreement with Russia was purely pragmatic – he needed to ensure the destruction of Poland without any outside interference. The British and French guarantees to Poland were useless without Soviet support, and Hitler believed that they would have no alternative but to accept Germany's demands.

The outbreak of war

Hitler was shocked at the British announcement of a formal military alliance with Poland on 25 August. He ordered his generals to postpone the Polish invasion planned to start the next day. Some historians believe that a second Munich-style agreement might have been possible at this point, especially as Mussolini had informed Hitler that Italy would be unable to go to war in the event of a general conflict. Hitler made an offer of talks to Chamberlain on 27 August, saying he would guarantee the British Empire in return for a negotiated settlement to the Polish–German dispute. Talks between Germany and Poland were renewed on 28 August, but Hitler had already ordered a new invasion date of 1 September. Also, the Polish government rejected any concessions over the question of Danzig, unlike the Czechs in 1938, so making a second Munich impossible.

Hitler's excuse for invasion was an alleged Polish attack on a German radio station near the border. SS men dressed in Polish army uniforms massacred 'German' villagers – these were really concentration camp inmates. The German invasion began at dawn on 1 September, Hitler claiming to the German public that German troops had been returning Polish fire.

Source 13.2

German troops smashing Polish border barriers, 1939

Yet Britain and France waited 48 hours before declaring war on Germany. Chamberlain was hoping to get Mussolini to persuade Hitler to agree to last-minute talks, but the attempt was unsuccessful because of British and French insistence on German withdrawal of troops from Poland. Once again, Chamberlain was trying as much as possible to rescue his appeasement policy, even at the very last minute.

At 11.15am on Sunday 3 September 1939, Chamberlain made a radio broadcast announcing Britain's declaration of war. At noon, he made a statement to parliament, which clearly showed the personal investment he had in appeasement:

> This a sad day for all of us, and none is it sadder than to me. Everything that I have worked for, everything that I have hoped for, everything that I have believed in during my public life, has crashed into ruins. There is only one thing left for me to do; that is, to devote what strength and powers I have to forwarding the victory of the cause for which we have to sacrifice so much. I cannot tell what part I may be allowed to play myself; I trust I may live to see the day when Hitlerism has been destroyed and a liberated Europe has been re-established.
>
> Neville Chamberlain, Statement to the House of Commons,
> September 3 1939

Chamberlain continued as Prime Minister until May 1940, but died of cancer in November of the same year. He did not live to see Europe liberated.

Activity

1 Look at **Source 13.1** and the text. What areas of dispute were there between Germany and Poland, and how had Poland's position worsened after Munich?

2 Why could it be argued that the British guarantee to Poland was illogical? Think about:

- the geographical position of Poland; the ethnic make-up of the disputed territories

- Chamberlain's previous actions.

3 'A missed opportunity.' Discuss this view of the negotiations for an alliance between Britain and the Soviet Union in summer 1939.

4 Why did Hitler and Stalin agree to a Non-Aggression Pact in August 1939?

Source question practice

Source A

Source 13.3

A French cartoon from spring 1939 – The Fox and the Grapes. Hitler has already taken grapes marked Austria, Czechoslovakia and Memel, and is looking up at ones marked Yugoslavia, Romania and Danzig.

Source B

I must confess to a most profound distrust of Russia. I have no belief whatever in her ability to maintain an effective offensive, even if she wanted to. And I distrust her motives which seem to me to have little connection with our ideas of liberty, and to be concerned only with getting everyone else by the ears. Moreover, she is hated and suspected by the smaller states, notably Poland, Romania and Finland.

From Chamberlain's diary, 26 March 1939

1 To what extent does **Source A** explain the change in British and French policy after March 1939?

Use the source and recalled knowledge.

2 How fully does **Source B** explain Chamberlain's attitude to an Anglo–Soviet alliance in 1939?

Use the source and recalled knowledge.

The Polish Crisis and the outbreak of World War Two

Appeasement: right or wrong?

Introduction

Throughout this book, different opinions about appeasement have been outlined and explained. The policy is as controversial now as it was then. Appeasement in Britain since 1940 has been a word that is used negatively. Yet in many ways, the policy of appeasement can be defended, as we have seen.

To understand how this situation came about, the historiography of appeasement will be examined in this final chapter. This will perhaps allow the reader to arrive at a balanced judgement rather than the knee-jerk response of 'appeasement is always wrong'.

The 'Guilty Men'

During and immediately after World War Two, appeasement was viewed by most people as a disastrous policy. British popular opinion was perhaps summed up by the publication in 1940 of *Guilty Men* by a group of left-wing journalists known collectively as 'Cato'. The book was a denunciation of Chamberlain and his policy. In the words of Frank McDonough, a modern historian of the policy, the book:

> …portrays appeasement as a combination of calculated deception, incompetent leadership, diplomatic bungling and extremely poor military planning.
>
> *Frank McDonough, Hitler, Chamberlain and Appeasement, 2002*

By the time the book was published, Churchill had been appointed Prime Minister, and although there were many political differences between the authors and Churchill, their views on appeasement were similar. In the words of another historian:

> *Guilty Men* proved that Churchill had been right all along, that Hitler had been hell-bent on aggression from the outset, just as he had long been saying.
>
> *Philip M Taylor, 'Appeasement: Guilty Men or Guilty Conscience?', Modern History Review, November 1989*

This remained the typical view until the 1960s, fuelled by knowledge of what the war led to, such as the Holocaust. Historians such as John Wheeler-Bennett and politicians, including Churchill himself, who published his massive six-volume *History of the Second World War* between 1948 and 1954, portrayed Chamberlain as a poor leader who was fooled by Hitler. As wartime Prime Minister, Churchill's views carried massive weight, and when he stated that appeasement was doomed to failure when pursued from a position of military weakness, few people were prepared to challenge this.

Many other memoirs from politicians, diplomats, military chiefs and journalists, published in the 1950s and early 1960s, tended to back up these opinions.

- Chamberlain was a weak and incompetent leader.
- He and his government failed to understand the true nature of Nazism.
- Britain was militarily weak, so appeasement was bound to fail.
- Chamberlain and his government deceived the British public, especially at Munich.

AJP Taylor's *Origins of the Second World War*

This book was published in 1961, and while it concentrated more on Hitler than Chamberlain, it did stimulate debate on the causes of the war. Taylor viewed Hitler as not much different from other German leaders, in aiming for German domination of Europe. Where Chamberlain came in for criticism was in his policy which seemed to fall over backwards to make concessions to Hitler. In Taylor's view, the Second World War was caused as much by the mistakes of Chamberlain and other democratic leaders as by the policies of the dictators. Other historians challenged Taylor's opinions, although not because of what he wrote about Chamberlain. They were concerned at Taylor's portrayal of Hitler as just another conventional German leader, rather than a totalitarian mass murderer. The 'guilty men' idea was still unchallenged.

Revisionism

In 1967, the Labour government of Harold Wilson allowed historians access to key government documents under the '30-year rule'. Previously, the archives had been closed for 50 years. Now, the minutes of Cabinet meetings and government papers from the 1930s were open to historians and the thinking and information behind many of the decisions could be scrutinised. The result was an explosion of books and articles on British foreign policy in the 1930s, which challenged the traditional view of

appeasement. Now Chamberlain was seen, not as a weak and useless incompetent, but as a realistic and able politician, keenly aware of the Nazi danger. While it is difficult to summarise the views of the revisionists, there are perhaps three main reasons why Chamberlain pursued the policy of appeasement, according to Frank McDonough.

- **British economic weakness.** The country was recovering slowly from the trauma of the Depression, and would find it difficult to rearm quickly, as there would not be enough skilled workers.
- **British military and naval weakness.** This had been apparent before (during the Manchurian and Abyssinian crises), but Chamberlain took careful note of warnings from army and navy chiefs that Britain was simply not ready to fight a war against Germany, Italy and Japan at the same time. Evidence can be seen earlier in this book.
- **Public opinion.** This was opposed to large-scale rearmament, certainly before 1937, and was anxious to avoid war.

> *In the light of these factors, appeasement was a logical policy choice which attempted to persuade Nazi Germany to live in peace with the rest of Europe before accepting that military force had to be used.*
>
> Frank McDonough, *Hitler, Chamberlain and Appeasement*, 2002

Revisionist historians such as David Dilks emphasise that Chamberlain, like other British leaders, accepted that the Treaty of Versailles should be revised. He also understood that Britain lacked the military strength to oppose German demands, at least in the short term.

Chamberlain also genuinely reflected what most British people felt about the prospect of another war – horror. But, this was not a policy of peace at any price, because the British government was following its traditional foreign policy of opposing any European power which tried to dominate the continent. If Hitler showed he could not be trusted, ultimately Britain would fight.

Other revisionist historians such as Maurice Cowling stress the importance of domestic policy. Appeasement made sense to the Conservative Party because it was popular with the voters and so could help them retain power in a general election, which would have to be held no later than 1940. Supported by John Charmley, Cowling argued that the policy should have continued in 1939. If it had, France would not have been defeated, and the British Empire preserved from destruction. Britain would have continued to be a great power.

These revisionist arguments are rather hypothetical, and are also driven by their authors' political opinions as supporters of the modern Conservative Party.

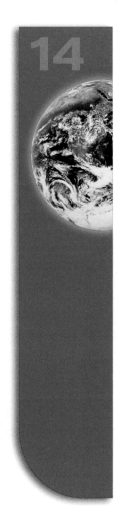

In evaluating the views of revisionist historians, it is also important to remember that many of their works depend too much on official documents. These would be written by people who tended to support the government policy of appeasement at the time, so in themselves do not give the full picture. There is little awareness of the importance of public opinion outside parliament, and political opposition within it. There is also not much discussion of intelligence reports, which gave the government invaluable information about Nazi plans. We know that Chamberlain and his advisers were fully aware of these reports, which mostly showed that Hitler's ambitions stretched far beyond a simple revision of Versailles.

So, while we can criticise the 'guilty men' thesis for being overly dependent on selective memory and guilt and shame at what seemed to be moral cowardice, the revisionists have been equally selective in the other direction. They base many of their judgements on an over-reliance on official documents and, at least in some cases, on nostalgia for the British Empire.

Post-revisionism

More recent works on the subject have given us perhaps a more balanced evaluation of appeasement. Even amid an avalanche of revisionist literature, there have been historians who continued to be critical of Chamberlain. Keith Middlemass, working from the same official sources, came to radically different conclusions in his 1972 book *The Diplomacy of Illusion: the British government and Germany 1937–1939*. Middlemass avoided any moral criticisms of Chamberlain, but criticised him for poor judgement, planning and timing. The 'illusion' of the title was Chamberlain's stubborn belief that Hitler's demands could be satisfied by revision of Versailles and a series of personal meetings and written agreements.

RAC Parker, writing in 1993, puts forward what is described as a 'counter-revisionist' theory. This accepts that Chamberlain was able and clear-sighted, but rejects the revisionist view that appeasement was followed because of economic and military weakness. Parker argues that Chamberlain rejected alternatives and followed appeasement stubbornly. This clouded his judgement about Hitler's intentions, leading him to believe that he was an essentially reasonable man.

The revisionists possibly went too far in their rehabilitation of Chamberlain, and the evidence suggests that he ignored advice which did not fit in with his aims. In very modern fashion, he surrounded himself with his own inner circle of advisers who told him only what he wanted to hear. McDonough describes it as 'a crisis management strategy – not a fully worked out foreign policy.'

The final analysis

Your task in preparing for the examination is to show awareness of these views, but also to have a secure knowledge and understanding of the key events. It is important to remember that appeasement stretched back to 1919, when many people in Britain were critical of the Versailles settlement. British foreign policy towards Germany in the 1920s was conciliatory, often disagreeing with France, for example over the Ruhr crisis of 1923 (see Chapter 2). This conflict and rivalry worsened after Hitler came to power.

Finally, it is important to beware the benefit of hindsight. Because we know that Hitler was a genocidal mass murderer who was primarily responsible for a war in which 50 million people died, it is easy now to say that politicians such as Macdonald, Baldwin and Chamberlain should have acted differently. But was this clear to people at the time?

What can be stated with confidence now is that AJP Taylor's view that the outbreak of war in 1939 was as much the fault of British and French leaders as that of Hitler has been discredited by the work of recent historians such as Richard Overy and Ian Kershaw. The consensus is now that the Second World War broke out largely because of Hitler's aggressive foreign policy, fuelled by the Nazi ideology of racism and living space. It is in the light of this knowledge that the policy of appeasement has to be considered.

Index